D0683944

# THE
# PEOPLE'S
# CHURCH

To Mary Hogan Berwick

Geppi buaj IS beautiful

Gary

Austin TX 3 - 96.

TABASCO

VERACRUZ

Palenque •

Amatán •

Simojovel •

OAXACA

Bochil • Larraínzar • Chilón-Bachajón •

Chamula • Oxchuc • Ocosingo •

Tenejapa

Tuxtla Gutiérrez • Zinacantán Altamirano •

San Cristóbal

Las Margaritas

Comitán •

Soconusco Valley

GUATEMALA

PACIFIC OCEAN

Tapachula •

0        km        100

MEXICO

# CHIAPAS

# THE PEOPLE'S CHURCH

## BISHOP SAMUEL RUIZ OF MEXICO
## AND WHY HE MATTERS

### GARY MacEOIN

*A Crossroad Book*
The Crossroad Publishing Company
New York

1996

The Crossroad Publishing Company
370 Lexington Avenue, New York, NY 10017

Copyright © 1996 by Gary MacEoin

All rights reserved. No part of this book may be reproduced, stored in a retrieval system, or transmitted, in any form or by any means, electronic, mechanical, photocopying, recording, or otherwise, without the written permission of The Crossroad Publishing Company.

Printed in the United States of America

---

**Library of Congress Cataloging-in-Publication Data**

MacEóin, Gary, 1909–
    The people's church : Bishop Samuel Ruiz of Mexico and why he matters / Gary MacEóin.
        p. cm.
    Includes bibliographical references and index.
    ISBN 0-8245-1576-5
    1. Ruiz García, Samuel. 2. Chiapas (Mexico).—History—Peasant Uprisings, 1994– 3. Ejército Zapatista de Liberación Nacional (Mexico) 4. Mexico—Politics and government—1988– 5. Catholic Church. Diocese of Chiapas (Mexico) 6. Church work with the poor—Catholic Church—History—20th century. 7. Christianity and politics. 8. Church and state. I. Title.
F1256.R85M3    1996
972'.75–dc20                                                                      95-49788
                                                                                      CIP

# CONTENTS

# INTRODUCTION

P EOPLE who tuned in to Ocosingo's regional radio station, XEOCH, early in the morning of New Year's Day 1994 quickly realized that a new era was dawning in Chiapas, Mexico's most southerly state. The lively *música ranchera* was interrupted by individuals named "Ovidio," "Uno," and "Virginia." Each repeated the same announcement. The Zapatista National Liberation Army (EZLN) had risen in arms, demanding the ouster of the Mexican president and repudiating the North American Free Trade Agreement (NAFTA), a "death certificate for the indigenous peoples of Mexico who are regarded as expendable by the government of Carlos Salinas de Gortari." The treaty was scheduled to come into effect that very day.

The Zapatista uprising vaulted Chiapas into the national and international headlines. With that symbolic statement by the masked Subcomandante Marcos, the long silent and powerless indigenous peoples took control of their own lives and their own future. Regardless of the setbacks that the immediate future might bring, a historic bridge had been crossed.

The instinctive response of the Mexican government, the Mexican armed forces, and the Chiapan power brokers was one of outrage. The reaction was not only of outrage, however, but also of subconscious fear. It was clear that the Zapatistas had gone almost completely unnoticed for several years as they trained their troops and developed a sophisticated organization. This was no hastily assembled collection

1

of desperate people hoping to attract support by taking arms. They already had a mass base and a well thought out project.

As one can see with hindsight, the Zapatista uprising followed logically from the new mood of the indigenous peoples of the Americas that developed in response to the commemoration in 1992 of the fifth centenary of the arrival of Europeans to this continent. As the indigenous began to speak openly of "invasion" rather than "conquest," it became evident that they had never accepted as final their military defeat. It was also becoming obvious that all the efforts of the European invaders to eliminate the original inhabitants of the continent as a social force had not succeeded. Indigenous people speaking their own languages and living within their own cultures could no longer be dismissed as numerically and socially irrelevant. Far from disappearing, they have rapidly increased their numbers in the second half of the twentieth century: fifteen million in Mexico, four or five times as many in all the Americas. After having been nearly wiped out by the fifteenth-century invasion, down to ten million sixty years later, they are today probably as many as they were in 1492. And they are asserting ever more insistently that this is their land.

The Zapatistas also differed in their stated aims from the perennial revolts in Mexico of those excluded from the benefits of the society. Their objective, they insisted, was not to replace the existing government and impose a new political and social system. What they wanted was merely to provide the political space that would enable all Mexicans to participate in the creation of a just society. They were not committed to asserting exclusive control and ownership over the entire continent. They were simply asking to be recognized as having the same rights and dignity as the other inhabitants.

Without using the technical vocabulary, they expressed the philosophy of liberation theology and of the Christian base communities that have proliferated in Latin America since the 1960s. They called, not for vertical structures with themselves at the top of the pyramid, but for horizontal structures in which all would share power. They wanted a government that would be accountable to the people and would give effective representation and participation to all Mexicans, including the hitherto excluded indigenous.

For a society in which one party, the Party of the Institutionalized Revolution (PRI), had monopolized all power at the national, state, and local levels for more than half a century, this was a challenging proposal. The uprising was thus placed in a very specific historical context: it was a response to the restructuring of the capitalist system on a global scale, and a challenge to the always fragile legitimacy of the Mexican state.

❖

Rather than face up to the challenge, the first response of the Mexican government — through its controlled media — was to discover a scapegoat. Samuel Ruiz García, bishop of San Cristóbal de Las Casas, was the sole and exclusive cause of the outbreak, they insisted. God's guerrilla, they screamed, Zapatista *comandante*, the Pol Pot of Chiapas.

In a very real sense, though not in the way they presented it, they were right. Don Samuel, as he is universally known and greeted, had done more than anyone else in the history of Chiapas to prepare its long oppressed people to assert their rights. Not that he ever had political ambitions or a political agenda. He simply had heard the cry of the people and had accepted his role as bishop to lead them to integral liberation.

When he arrived in San Cristóbal de Las Casas in 1960, Samuel Ruiz discovered a world that had largely remained suspended in time, a colonial-type society divided into social castes, where the rich were less rich than in other parts of the country but the poor were poorer, and relations between rich and poor were openly harsh because expressed in terms of race division.

In this completely new social atmosphere, the bishop started his work very modestly, encouraging people to take charge of their own lives at the most elementary level. But the logic of his approach forced him bit by bit to identify and challenge the structures of oppression that were central to the Mexican political system. His analysis of these structures had become and continues to be a threat to entrenched injustice. It brought him to question not only the political system but important figures in his own church who cooperated with and thus fortified that system. A venturesome David prepared to do battle with the two-headed Goliath of church and state.

January 1994 was by no means the first time that the bishop of San Cristóbal had been launched into the limelight. For many years he had been a controversial figure. He made no secret of his belief that the poor of Chiapas were "the victims of a structural situation of oppression" and that "if we take the gospel option, we have to dismantle the structures of domination." That commitment to the oppressed indigenous peoples of his diocese had long since won the hostility of the state government of Chiapas, the political party (PRI) that has monopolized power in all of Mexico for some sixty-five years, the cattle barons and businessmen of Chiapas, and the papal nuncio to Mexico, Archbishop Girolamo Prigione. Their identifying him as the source of this new trouble surprised nobody.

Within days, however, the tune changed. The reaction in Mexico to the Zapatista uprising was an unprecedented mobilization of civil society, of public opinion sympathetic to the demands of the rebels and insisting on a negotiated settlement. The charismatic figure of Subcomandante Marcos aroused sympathy for the movement in general. A kind of radical chic appeal reached broad sectors of the middle and upper classes who had never before so much as thought of the indigenous as fellow Mexicans. The guerrilla mystique, combined with the indigenous mystique and the massive coverage by the international media, frustrated the government's attempts to brand the Zapatistas as criminals led by foreigners. Reports of bombing of peaceful villages by military planes were followed by TV pictures of young men stretched face down in the marketplace of Ocosingo, which the army had occupied, their hands tied behind their backs and identical bullet wounds in their heads. The rebels might be no military threat, but they were way ahead in the war for hearts and minds.

The sympathetic reaction of public opinion and the overwhelming support — in Mexico and elsewhere — of the Zapatista demand for land and dignity caused intolerable embarrassment to the government. A precipitous plunge of the stock market boded ill for the influx of foreign capital it had hoped would follow the coming into force of NAFTA. A car bomb explosion in Mexico City and explosions in four other states added to the alarm. The government quickly realized that the routine solution of massive force was unacceptable. It was left with no alternative but to appeal to the Pol Pot of Chiapas. Ruiz alone held the key to a solution.

He held it because he was not only the most hated person in Mexico. He was also the most beloved. The Zapatistas would accept no other go-between, and in consequence Don Samuel's enemies had to swallow their pride. He was the sole non-indigenous Mexican whom the indigenous trusted. A great compliment. His authority was such as to enable him in little more than a week to negotiate a cease-fire that, with one brief interruption, still holds.

❖

A striking example of the sophistication of the Zapatista leadership was its choice of language in communiqués. In the first days of the uprising, it directed its appeal to students and other activists of the Mexican left, using terms identified with the revolutionary movements of Latin America, Africa, and Asia, an abstract political and military language reminiscent of Frantz Fanon's *Les damnés de la terre* ("the wretched of the earth").

Within a short time, however, as soon as Mexican and world opinion had shown its solid support for the proclaimed objectives of the Zapatistas, the language changed.

One could now hear clearly the authentic voice of the long voiceless Mayans, the historical protest of a concrete indigenous people. "For many years we reaped the death of our children from the fields of Chiapas. Our children were killed by forces unknown to us. Our men and women walked the long night of ignorance.... The elders of our people had spoken to us words that came from far away, from a time when our lives were ours, when our voice was quiet. And truth walked in the words of the elders of our people when they told us that the long night of our suffering had come from the hands and words of the powerful."

Probably no such substantive dialogue had ever before taken place in any part of the world between the original inhabitants and the white invaders. And it could hardly have taken place now in Mexico were it not for the awakening of the indigenous people of Chiapas through the work of the diocese of San Cristóbal, and specifically of its organization of the 1974 Indigenous Congress and the 1986 general diocesan assembly (see below, p. 37). Throughout history, European explorers and missionaries were never able to appreciate the wisdom of indigenous peoples, many of whom — as in Mexico — were vastly more learned than their conquerors. With individual exceptions whose views never prevailed, they relied on power to achieve their purposes. And in Mexico, finally, the balance of power was shifting.

The Zapatistas insisted on the dignity of the indigenous, a dignity long denied by the conquerors. "This is why we rose...; we were forced to do it. We natives fight in order to have our dignity respected." They insisted on the need for action to survive: "...so that we can have decent housing, a reasonable job, land to cultivate." They insisted on the need for democratic institutions that alone allow community functioning. "The terrible conditions of poverty endured by our people have a single common cause: the lack of freedom and of democracy. We believe that any improvement in the economic and social circumstances of our country's poor requires a truly authentic respect for the people's freedom and democratic will."[1]

The sophistication of the Zapatista leadership was again demonstrated when the government followed up the cease-fire with an apparently conciliatory gesture: a vote of amnesty. The response gave a hint of the real depth of their demands, as well as of their political sophistication. In words that recall the justification offered by the signatories of the U.S. Declaration of Independence for rebelling against George III, they said they rejected an amnesty because they had committed no crime by revolting against an illegitimate government. "Who must ask for forgiveness and who can give it," Marcos answered sarcastically. "For what must we ask forgiveness? For refusing to die of hunger? Who must ask for forgiveness and who can give it? The president of the Republic? The senators? The deputies? The governors? The municipal presidents? The police? The federal army? The owners of banks, industry, commerce, and land? The political parties? The intellectuals? ... The mass media? The teachers? The urban poor? The workers? The campesinos? The indigenous? Those who died such useless deaths? Who must ask for forgiveness and who can give it?"[2]

The Zapatistas had another valid reason for their stand. They did not want an amnesty that would pardon the crimes committed by the Mexican armed forces against the civilian population in the days preceding the cease-fire. The amnesty device had been widely used in Argentina, El Salvador, Guatemala, and elsewhere to allow military dictators and their death squads to escape punishment for their misdeeds. The Zapatistas were already charging the Mexican army with systematic violations of human rights, charges that subsequently were documented by the Canadian Catholic Organization for Development and Peace, Americas Watch, and Amnesty International.[3] The strategy of the military and police forces for ending social resistance is, according to Amnesty, to engage in the practice of torture, repression, coercion, injustice, extra-judicial executions, and death threats.[4]

What happened in Chiapas in 1994 makes sense only when seen in a national and a hemispheric context. It represents a new phase in what Spanish philosopher Ortega y Gasset called in the 1920s "the rebellion of the masses." That rebellion was marked in the 1970s and 1980s in Latin America — where the word *guerrilla* had originated — by armed revolts that would in many cases have toppled the system of institutionalized injustice (as the Catholic bishops of Latin America defined it at Medellín in 1968) were it not for external intervention: U.S. military might, aided and ideologically justified by the doctrine of national security.

For a moment in early 1994 the Zapatista uprising seemed nothing more than an anachronistic echo of those frustrated guerrilla approaches to liberation. That it represented a fundamentally different phenomenon, however, quickly became apparent. The arms of the Zapatistas were merely a diversion, no more a threat to the system than Don Quixote's lance and cardboard helmet. No. The threat was more discreet, also more dangerous. What Don Samuel has called *la Señora Sociedad Civil* ("lady civil society") was emerging on the public scene. Instead of violence, it offered a more radical challenge to the institutionalized disorder: the peaceful, legal mobilization of people.

The importance of active participation of civil society in dealing with social unrest was stressed by Don Samuel in his 1994 Lenten pastoral letter.[5] The point may seem obvious to outsiders, but the reality of Mexico is that governments under the long-established one-party system had routinely ignored public opinion in their decision-making. "The armed uprising in Chiapas and the misguided official response to it," the bishop wrote, "created such a level of tension in the first days that it was at the point of sending the entire country up in flames, with an escalation of irrational and generalized violence. Thanks to God and to the timely intervention of sensible people — and above all, to the intervention of *civil society*, which made its appearance with a unanimous commitment to negotiation — the spiral of violence was halted."

This new understanding of civil society as a political actor, which is being widely debated and analyzed in Mexico today, has emerged in Latin America over the past thirty years, having developed in step with the Christian base community movement, of which it can be described as the civil counterpart. Indeed it makes sense to see the two movements as a response to the same social situation: the failure of existing institutions to provide the overwhelming majority of their constituents with the supports that are the raison d'être of these institutions.

In their first communiqué on New Year's Day 1994, the Zapatistas took the high ground by insisting that they were not rebelling against the Mexican state but challenging usurpers who were violating the federal Constitution. "In adherence to the Constitution," they declared, "we issue this Declaration of War against the Federal Mexican Army, key pillar of the dictatorship headed illegally by its highest and illegitimate leader — Salinas."[6]

In that same communiqué they described the essence of the new phenomenon that they represented. "A slow accumulation of forces" had taken place in silence, it said, a process that had grown out of the "independent organizations" of the people. What had happened was that the people had given up on the political parties that had consistently sold them short. They had decided instead to develop community at the grass roots, to forget about high-level political fantasies and concentrate on local needs: schools, clinics, sewers, public transport for people and goods, and especially land.

As with the base communities, the individual units coalesced into networks. They called them unions, alliances, blocs, coordinating committees, convergences, fronts. The networks grew into Unions of Unions that could mobilize tens of thousands and threaten a situation of ungovernability. Some of them had been infiltrated or split by the co-optationist policies of the authorities. But within days of the Zapatista proclamation, 700 delegates of the 280 Chiapan organizations that formed the State Council of Indigenous and Campesino Organizations (CEOIC) unanimously supported the EZLN rejection of the government proposals.

❖

This new concept of civil society has been growing everywhere in Latin America, especially since it became clear that the U.S. veto had made the guerrilla approach to liberation unviable for the foreseeable future. It was no accident, however, that it first achieved national recognition in the diocese of San Cristóbal. For more than two decades this diocese, under the guidance of Bishop Ruiz, had been laying the groundwork. The motivation of its initiatives was purely pastoral, but its proclaimed objective of integral liberation, from sin and from oppression, caused it to affect all aspects of the lives of the people. The following chapters will describe how this came about.

In March 1994, Don Samuel — by then accepted as negotiator between the Zapatistas and the federal government — took advantage of the already mentioned Lenten pastoral letter[7] to put on the record what in his opinion had provoked the Zapatista uprising and what radical changes would be needed in Mexico to resolve the problems it had identified. Some weeks earlier, he had already clarified that the pastoral work of the diocese had not been the only factor in the awakening of the indigenous people who had taken up arms. "The left-wing political groups who came to Chiapas from Torreón [following the 1968 student protests in Mexico City and elsewhere]," he said, "took advantage of the religious infrastructure created by the diocese of San Cristóbal de Las Casas, and they carried on their activities in the highlands and in the Lacandon jungle with a discourse that was not only Marxist but even atheistic."

Following his well-established didactic technique, Don Samuel opened the pastoral letter with a formulation of the situation as he saw it, and then set out his interpretation of the events in the light of the Christian message. The Zapatistas, he wrote, "are simply our indigenous brothers and sisters and poor campesinos of the highlands of Chiapas who, after long suffering, reached the desperate decision that no way was open to them other than to demand their rights, with arms in their hands, accepting the risk of perishing in the attempt. They themselves insist that their leadership consists principally of indigenous campesinos, although there are also non-indigenous people who support their cause. They are not outsiders or 'professionals of violence.' "

As for their ideology, the bishop said it was not easy to define. "They do not seem very concerned about ideology. Their communiqués reveal a mixture of nationalism and various kinds of socialism. What is fundamental to their struggle is the meeting of very concrete demands whose common denominator is the call for justice for the poor. That is perhaps the very reason that their voice has had such impact, for it has been understood and accepted as the rebellion of both the indigenous and non-indigenous people excluded from the system."

Although many at first had made sarcastic comments about their wooden guns, it gradually emerged that they possessed a discipline and an intelligent grasp of military strategies that astonished even the Mexican army. "Nevertheless, the major strength of the EZLN is not so much in their arms or their military strategy as in the ability they have shown to create sympathy for their cause in civil society. In a manner of speaking, this has gradually transformed them not only into catalysts but also into spokespersons for the generalized discontent of civil society with the 'established order.' Their proposals are suggestive rather than assertive, so that all of us feel challenged by them."

The bishop's moral evaluation of the decision of the Zapatistas to resort to armed struggle is particularly noticeable. "As messengers of the peace announced by the One born in Bethlehem, our diocesan church cannot justify the recourse to violence as an ordinary means for solving the serious and deep-rooted problems of the region. This we expressed clearly both before and at the beginning of the conflict.

Nevertheless, to the extent that we as pastors are interpreters for our people and share their hopes, we understand the anguish and prolonged suffering of our brothers and sisters that drove them to the subjective conclusion that all peaceful ways had been closed to them."

Turning to an evaluation of the response of the Mexican armed forces to the uprising, the bishop said that once the "social order" had been broken by the EZLN's declaration of war, the intervention of the armed forces to restore the social order was necessary. The form in which they intervened was, however, unacceptable. "On the basis of evidence gathered by our church and confirmed by the media and both national and international NGOs, the Mexican army has gone beyond its proper function by violations of the human rights both of those who had taken up arms and of the civilian population. These violations, committed by those obligated by constitutional mandate to guarantee the safety of all Mexicans, offend not only the image of the army but the national conscience. For that reason, they should be investigated and punished appropriately in order to clear the image of the armed forces in the mind of civil society.... Incidents resulting from the action of the EZLN have produced a negative reaction in the national consciousness, but incidents attributed to the Mexican army have had a far greater negative impact on public opinion. It is said that the army kidnapped suspected members of the EZLN and executed not only prisoners taken in battle but civilians."

After this down-to-earth description of the events, Don Samuel moves to an equally candid presentation of what should be the pastoral response. "This complex reality raises for Christians and their pastors serious questions and challenges as to how we should understand them in the light of our faith and how we can respond appropriately to them. Some reflections will help us to place the facts in the concrete context in which they occurred.

"Chiapas is one of the most impoverished states of the Federation, not because it lacks natural resources for its development — on the contrary, it has them in abundance — nor because the majority of its people are indigenous, but because it is saddled with unjust mechanisms of a model of production and accumulation of wealth that have systematically privileged a few at the expense of the majority. This structural situation is an 'institutionalized violence' that daily offends social coexistence and constitutes the culture in which all political or armed popular revolts breed.

"The church, when faced with this violence of the 'established order,' cannot remain silent lest it condone by its silence the sin of the world. With the energy that the spirit of the prophets has given us, and with the power of the gospel, we have called — in season and out of season — for the conversion of persons and of social structures. But it would seem that we have been 'a voice crying in the wilderness.'...

"The situation in Chiapas has become even more complicated in recent years, and that for a simple reason. The gains of the Mexican Revolution — land reform, public health, social justice, effective suffrage, and free education — never reached this state. Now the indigenous see the structural adjustment promoted by the present administration to ensure the integration of Mexico into the capitalist bloc of the North, giving facilities to private investors for greater access to our agricultural resources, as the government's total abandonment of the common people. They also see it as the government's open alliance with the moneyed elements who have robbed and with impunity continue to rob them of their land and its produce.

"The reasoning of these indigenous campesinos is very simple. If in the previous circumstances, in which the popular or populist directives of the Mexican Revolution prevailed, the poor in Chiapas were unable to obtain their demands, what can they hope for now that the legal framework openly favors the wealthy? The sense of hopelessness that hit them has made a profound impression on their lives....

"The armed uprising of the indigenous of the Chiapan highlands has shown first of all that the Mexican state has

still a historical debt to pay to those who are the oldest social base of the nation, namely, the indigenous peoples. They
have not been taken into account in practical terms in any
of the country's projects implemented by one government after another in the course of our history. What is worse, they
have often been seen as excess population or an obstacle to
our national development. From a global perspective, the indigenous people have been the forgotten, the downtrodden,
or the marginated ones. They are in actual fact 'strangers in
their own land.'

"When they have been mentioned in national plans, it is
mostly as a social stain that should be wiped out, a historical
past to be put in books, or a folkloric present to be protected
for the pleasure of international tourism. This is the greatest
social sin, one for which all of us should beg pardon. It is a
historical error that those who have taken up arms throw in
our face, one that we have to correct unequivocally.

"We cannot continue to build the future of Mexico on
the grave of the indigenous peoples, neglecting to incorporate seriously the oldest root of our national identity and
failing to give today's descendants of the first people to forge
our Motherland the worthy place to which they are entitled.
But in addition to making us tragically aware of the historical exclusion of the indigenous from our national project,
the occurrences in Chiapas also show the level of generalized
discontent present in civil society, not only because of this exclusion, but because of the very blueprint that is being applied
to the country. For the critical conscience of civil society, not
only is there no place for the indigenous, but equally no place
for broader sectors of the poor and of both rural and urban
workers.

"The explosion of indigenous desperation has been the cat-
alyzer of the general discontent of the other social sectors.
That is why Chiapas acquired so quickly the solidarity of
groups so far away and so different. The awareness of not
being taken into account in the building of modern Mexico
has unified in Chiapas the wish to tell those who are running

the country that it is not right to take into account only a few
Mexicans — judged 'the most productive' — when projecting
the future of the nation, leaving to the rest no option save to
accept this as the only possible solution.

"For that reason, the most serious issue now is not just the
dialogue to reach a peaceable settlement between the government and the EZLN. Solution of the armed conflict will not
end the nation's serious problems. In the final analysis, we
still must find a solution for the dissatisfaction of civil society
as regards the proposed content and form of the country that
we all have to build. Mexico cannot be the same after what
has happened in Chiapas.

"This is the moment of major corrections not only in
relation to the indigenous peoples, but in relation to all Mexicans. All of us are viscerally challenged to be creative so that
we can design the new Motherland we want. Nobody should
be excluded, no matter how apparently insignificant....

"To seek peace in the present circumstances is not simply
to ask the EZLN to put down arms so that we can return to
the old established order. We must undertake the building of
new networks of interpersonal relations, networks based on
justice and true solidarity. Concretely speaking, this involves
for the most favored sectors the renunciation of systems of
power and privilege based on disregard for human values and
on the legalized plundering of the indigenous communities. It
involves the return of the land that these communities know
was stolen from them. It involves the implementation of development projects and programs that give a higher priority
to the interests of the communities than to the level of profit
or of economic or political viability. The best return for any
public or private investment must be the human return, the
maintenance of peace and social concord....

"Chiapas has shown us how great is the power of reason
to contain violence and to open roads to life and to lasting peace. In this, civil society has been a principal factor
in establishing the conditions for dialogue and the political
negotiation of our conflicts. This critical conscience and this

citizen activism must be kept fully alive. It is essential not only for bringing to a favorable conclusion the dialogue between the parties to the conflict, but for assuring the just application of the agreements and for opening up political ways for all to participate in the building of the new Mexico that will eradicate the structural causes of violence, regardless of their origin, and will respond to our ancestral and legitimate longings as a people.

"This is what we Christians understand as the Easter experience, that is to say, to pass as persons and as a people from death to life by placing ourselves structurally on the road to historical resurrection.... Undoubtedly those who are opposed to the creation of a new Mexico that will not only be modern but will act justly toward all Mexicans will do everything in their power to render unfruitful the efforts for peace and justice to which we are committed. Perhaps they do not realize that it is God they are resisting, since the project of the poor is in the final analysis the project of God. For that reason we must stay alert to denounce the machinations of the Evil One. But we also have to be ready to pay, with dignity and Christian courage, the cost in sorrow and suffering that we undoubtedly will have to pay for the building of peace. Let us not forget that the resurrection is reached by enduring the suffering and cross of Calvary. As followers of Jesus, we do not seek martyrdom, but if it comes, we accept it as the ultimate demand of love for our brothers and sisters."

This 1994 Lenten pastoral letter written at a time when the bishop was involved day and night in negotiations that, as the letter makes clear, were for him of supreme importance for the future of Chiapas and of Mexico, is a tribute to his clear thinking, his ability to see through details to the essence of the problem, his fearless commitment to say exactly what he thinks, to speak truth to power. Here in this remote backwater, bypassed by progress, he presents himself as the voice of the long voiceless who now demand a radical rewriting of history. This statement alone suffices to ensure Samuel Ruiz a place in Mexican history.

❖

Although inhabited by humans for ten thousand years, San Cristóbal is hardly the place one would choose to embark on such a quixotic crusade as that envisaged in the bishop's manifesto. From the time of the creation of the diocese by Pope Paul III as Ciudad Real in 1539, clerics assigned there as bishop felt they were being punished, and most set out immediately to cultivate friends in high places who would secure their transfer to more attractive pastures. A map maker in 1540 located Ciudad Real in the center of a big island off the coast of Japan. Most Mexicans think of it as part of Guatemala, as it was in the original political carving up of the continent by the Spaniards, and as it still is culturally. The first Mexican president ever to visit it was Lázaro Cárdenas. That was in 1940, and although the distance is only five hundred miles, it took him four days to get there from Mexico City, traveling by sea, rail, and automobile. The Pan-American Highway, the first direct road, reached San Cristóbal only in 1946. Even today the journey is still an adventure.

The road from Tuxtla Gutiérrez, capital of the state of Chiapas, rises steeply as it clings to the side of precipices and snakes through mountain passes. The vivid red of the flamboyants in the lowlands soon gives way to forests of oak and pine. Rocky outcroppings mark eroded stretches of cutaway woodland that will take thousands of years to recover. Barefoot women with weatherbeaten faces, wearing red shawls and embroidered dresses, plod stolidly upward, almost doubled under loads of firewood. Military checkpoints presage arrival at the sleepy colonial city located 2,100 meters (6,890 feet) above sea level.

In the plaza in front of the cathedral, barefoot indigenous women, with babies on their backs and children clinging to their skirts, display for tourists the bracelets, blouses, and belts that are the traditional handicrafts of the Tzotziles and Tzeltales of the Chiapan highlands. It is to the people of these highlands that Don Samuel has devoted his life since he was named bishop of San Cristóbal in November 1959.

I have made the journey several times over a decade, and always with the same purpose: to get to know Don Samuel, and having known him, to get to know him better. He is eminently accessible, his door always open to the stream of people who come to seek his advice and help. His office and the two rooms that are his "home" are in the massive building attached to the left side of the cathedral. Usually dressed in a business suit, he welcomes visitors at all hours of the day and night. His enormous energy is at the service of a brilliant mind that switches effortlessly from issue to issue. At ease in every situation, he is equally attentive to the weak and the powerful. Withal, he is a man of prayer, always finding time to withdraw and reflect. As his secretary told me, "He prays much and sleeps little."

A stout friend. A formidable adversary.

# Chapter 1

# ROOTS OF GRACE

SYMBOLIC of the new self-image of the indigenous of the Chiapan highlands was an event at the ancient Mayan cultural and religious center of Palenque in March 1994. Traditional religious leaders of the five major language groups of the highlands of Chiapas, the Tzotzil, Tzeltal, Tojolabal, Chol, and Mam, climbed the steps of the Temple of Inscriptions, in which Lord Pacal was entombed fifteen hundred years ago. There they set up a shrine with multicolored candles and wild plants, burned copal incense, and invoked the aid of Lord Pacal to bring peace.

They then announced that the Fifth Sun, which in the Mayan calendar was identified as an age of hunger and disease, had set. It was time to welcome the Sixth Sun, an era of dawning hope and unity for the indigenous peoples.[8]

The immediate motivation for this proclamation was, of course, the Zapatista uprising that had taken the Mexican government by surprise and captured the imagination of the entire world two months earlier. But that movement is intelligible only within the story of thirty-four years of pastoral work and community leadership of the bishop of San Cristóbal de Las Casas, Don Samuel Ruiz.

Who is this man who arouses such violent reactions? Although a recent governor of Chiapas once declared angrily that either he or Don Samuel would rule the state, meaning that there was not room for both of them, the bishop has never aspired to political leadership, much less encouraged armed insurrection. His exclusive ambition was always the salvation of the people entrusted to his spiritual care, an objective that gradually grew to encompass their integral liberation, that is to say, liberation both from sin and from subhuman living conditions. It is the crime that has won him his distinguished array of enemies.

Don Samuel has formulated his mission many times and, as his identification with his people grew, with ever increasing clarity. Typical is a statement he issued on Mission Day in 1988: "To speak of solidarity with the indigenous is to speak of solidarity in the face of ethnocide and genocide.... It is to struggle for their right to their own cultural expressions, to their own way of living, ... to ensure that their habitat is recognized, the land that belonged to them, ... their right to their style of work with its communitarian characteristics."

❖

If San Cristóbal was an unlikely locale for a major revision of history, the Samuel Ruiz who arrived there as bishop in January 1960 was an equally unlikely catalyst for such a historic transformation. His previous ecclesiastical career provided no hint of what was to come. It was Pope John XXIII who ordained him bishop and sent him to San Cristóbal. Given the realities of ecclesiastical bureaucracy, it is extremely unlikely that John had more than a formal role in choosing him for this assignment. Yet one would like to think that this wise and godly man had some special insight from the Holy Spirit in making a decision with such transcendental consequences.

Samuel was the first of five children in a family of modest means from Irapuato in the state of Guanajuato. Guadalupe García, his mother, was orphaned at the age of eleven, worked as a maid for a rich family, and later moved to California. There she met and married Maclovio Ruiz Mejía, an agricultural worker also from Irapuato. Having decided they wanted their children to be Mexican, they returned in October 1924 to their home community and acquired a small plot of land, on which they built a house and a small grocery store. The project took several years and required several trips by Maclovio back to Arizona and California. All that existed when Samuel was born in November 1924 were two small rooms. Years later, when he was already a bishop, his mother confided that his father and she had given their first-born to God before his birth.

Having completed high school in the junior seminary at León, Samuel was sent to Rome to study philosophy and theology at the Gregorian University. In 1949 he was ordained to the priesthood. Then, after three further years of Scripture study in Rome and Jerusalem, he returned to the seminary at León as a professor. Soon he was named rector of the seminary and made a canon of the cathedral.

At this point everything prognosticated meteoric progress in ecclesiastical office. Canons of León were important people. Their purple capes edged with white ermine and their outsized rings seemed already to presage the cardinalate. And in fact preferment was not long in coming. At the age of thirty-five and only ten years a priest, Samuel was named bishop of San Cristóbal.

As one might anticipate from his training and experience, from which pastoral duties were notably absent, early actions as bishop included no surprises. His first pastoral letter focused on what was then the burning issue for churchmen in many lands. "Behind a creed that flaunts a banner of social justice, communism has been sneaking in falsehoods, hypocrisy, deceit, and calumny.... This campaign has already started in our country." In his choice of subject for this first message to his diocese, he was fully in line with the Mexican Bishops Conference, which about the same time responded to Fidel Castro's statement of commitment to socialism with a similar repudiation.

❖

The new bishop early made a decision, however, that was ultimately to change both him and his diocese radically. He set out on a mule to visit every town and village in the vast expanse over which he held jurisdiction. The diocese of San Cristóbal had encompassed the entire state of Chiapas, an area of 76,000 square kilometers (29,600 square miles) until a few years earlier when the northern part was cut off to form the diocese of Tuxtla Gutiérrez. What was left was a Pacific coast lowland region, mostly mestizo and Spanish-speaking, and the highlands, overwhelmingly indigenous and speaking many Mayan languages. Shortly after Don Samuel's arrival as bishop, the Pacific coastal region became the separate diocese of Tapachula, leaving him with the highlands.

What most impressed and shocked the bishop, as his mule carried him on tracks too narrow and rocky for a wheeled vehicle, up and down steep mountains, through forests of pine and oak in the highlands and tropical hardwoods in the Ocosingo Valley, was the poverty and abandonment in which the indigenous lived. It was something for which his previous experience had not prepared him. But it was something, he quickly concluded, that was essentially opposed to God's will for all humans.

His first formula for change for the highlands reflected the typical reaction of the outsider confronted with a different world. It was necessary to bring the indigenous into the twentieth century, he decided, meaning concretely to teach them Spanish and give them food and shoes. He began by enlisting the help of missionaries. Jesuits had been already at work in Bachajón-Chilón. In 1961 Franciscans established a base near Palenque. Dominicans from California came to Ocosingo in 1963. Maryknollers and lay missionaries also arrived. The diocese began to create rural cooperatives, health-care clinics, and credit unions for the indigenous.

Such initiatives were fully in tune with and the beneficiary of the prevailing attitudes toward Latin America. In 1961, Archbishop (later Cardinal) Agostino Casaroli appealed on behalf of the Pontifical Commission on Latin America to U.S. religious superiors to send 10 percent of their orders and congregations to Latin America. Simultaneously, the Peace Corps volunteers of the Alliance for Progress were promoting credit unions and cooperatives as the solution to the hemisphere's poverty.

It was all very positive, but it was still the traditional approach of the do-gooder who decides what is right for others without consulting them. The previous bishop of San Cristóbal, Lucio C. Torreblanca y Tapia, had made a start in the same direction. He had enlisted indigenous men and women to teach hymns and start question-and-answer catechism classes. Don Samuel enthusiastically accepted a suggestion of the apostolic delegate, Archbishop Luigi Raimondi, to open two schools to train indigenous men and women as catechists. The schools in a few years graduated seven hundred catechists.

The project was well intended, but its inadequacy was later recognized by the bishop in an August 1993 pastoral letter written on the occasion of Pope John Paul II's third visit to Mexico. "We have made many mistakes in our pastoral pilgrimage. Our first actions, before the Second Vatican Council, were destructive of culture. We had only our own — ethnocentric and moralistic — criteria to judge customs. Without realizing it, we were on the side of those who oppressed the indigenous."

Such self-analysis is typical of Don Samuel. It was helped by the Vatican Council (1962–65) and by the Second Conference of the Latin American Bishops (CELAM II) held in Medellín, Colombia, in 1968. Constant reflection on the results of decisions and actions is a continuing characteristic of his administration. It has carried him a long way from his original naive enthusiasm.

❖

For him, as for many, the Vatican Council was a watershed. There the bishops of Latin America, for the first time in history, spent long periods together and, under such inspired leaders as Dom Helder Camara (Recife, Brazil), Bishop Manuel Larraín (Talca, Chile), Bishop Sergio Méndez Arceo

(Cuernavaca, Mexico), and Bishop Leónidas Proaño (Riobamba, Ecuador), began to reflect on their problems in a
continental framework. The option for the poor as an in-
escapable element of the Christian commitment emerged as
a dominant theme. The longstanding practice of imposing
European forms in the evangelization of other cultures was
openly questioned.

A first fruit of the council in Mexico was the formation
in 1963 of the Bishops Mutual Aid Union (UMAE) by several bishops from poorer dioceses, one of whom was Don
Samuel. There he developed close ties with Ernesto Corripio
Ahumada, then bishop of Tampico, later archbishop in turn
of Oaxaca and Puebla, and cardinal primate of Mexico (retired in 1994). That friendship would prove valuable in the
aftermath of the Zapatista uprising.

In 1967 Ruiz became president of the Mexican Bishops
Committee on Indigenous Peoples (CEPI), a post he would
hold until 1974. Early in 1968 he attended a hemisphere-
wide discussion at Melgar, Colombia, preparatory to the
meeting of CELAM at Medellín later in the same year. The
theme of the meeting was missionary work in Latin America,
and it called for a new analysis from the perspective of their
cultures in working with indigenous peoples.

At Melgar, Don Samuel was elected president of CELAM's
Department of Missions, a position that he held until 1974
and that enabled him to expand the work of Mexico's
National Bishops Center for Aid to Indigenous Missions
(CENAMI) and to have the Center for Indigenous Pastoral
Work (CPI) created in 1970.

The historic meeting at Medellín, at which Latin America's bishops spelled out what the Vatican Council meant
for their hemisphere, carried the process further. Already
head of CELAM's Department of Missions, Don Samuel
incorporated Melgar's approach into a paper, which he delivered at the meeting, on adapting evangelization to the
Latin American context. He would continue to head this
CELAM department until 1972, when Archbishop (now Car-

dinal) Alfonso López Trujillo was elected secretary general and replaced all progressive department heads with his own conservative choices.

The 1960s had opened in a mood of worldwide euphoria. In the civil domain, it was typified by President John F. Kennedy's Alliance for Progress; in the religious, by Pope John XXIII's *Pacem in Terris* ("peace on earth"), a manifesto addressed not only to his co-religionists but to all people everywhere without distinction of sex, race, or belief.

By 1968 the mood had changed. At Medellín the Latin American bishops were denouncing the institutionalized violence of "the international monopolies and the international imperialism of money." The response to calls by the people of Czechoslovakia for justice and freedom was Russian tanks to smother Prague's brief spring. It was nightsticks and clubs to disperse rioting students in Paris and across Europe. It was baton charges and rifle fire against human rights marchers in Northern Ireland. It was a sniper's bullet to silence Martin Luther King's challenge to racism.

Mexico was no exception. On October 2, army troops and plainclothes police opened fire on several thousand unarmed students protesting police brutality and demanding the release of political prisoners. An unknown number, now believed to be at least several hundred, were killed. The place was Tlatelolco in Mexico City, the Plaza of the Three Cultures, pre-Hispanic, colonial, and modern. A symbolic event, it marked the end of Mexico's Revolution of 1910 and the integration of the Party of the Institutionalized Revolution (PRI) into the international structures of institutionalized violence. For decades to come its impact would reverberate more forcibly in the state of Chiapas and the diocese of San Cristóbal than anywhere else in Mexico. It would influence Samuel Ruiz's entire life.

❖

The distance the bishop had already traveled and the distance he had still to go can be measured by a later analysis of where he was in 1968. The catechists who had been trained in conventional catechesis, he wrote, were telling me that I had said good things about saving souls but had said nothing about saving bodies. They were describing the reality in which they and their communities lived: hungry, sick, poor, dying.

Their analysis helped us to understand better, he continued, what the Vatican Council and Medellín had said, namely, that the gospel is not just a collection of dogmas but a liberating proclamation and the practice of a new life. "This intensified our reflection and action on a catechesis that we called incarnational and that sought to clothe the Word of God in the flesh of the culture. The whole life of the community was revealed to us as a theological locus."[9]

The implementation of the new policy was no easy task. Three of every four people in the diocese are of Mayan origin and culture, and they speak seven different languages. The previous pastoral practice, in a diocese that covered the entire state of Chiapas and had few priests (only thirteen in 1960), was to station a priest in each major municipality. He visited the principal communities of the municipality from time to time, especially for the patronal feast. On such visits he stayed with the local boss, a landowner on whom every one in the community depended in one way or another. The people came to the big house to receive the sacraments, which for many meant only to have their children baptized.

Don Samuel followed this practice of staying at the big house when he made his first visitation of the diocese. With incisive self-criticism, he later recalled that first exposure to the reality of the life of the indigenous of Chiapas. "I was like a fish that sleeps with its eyes open. I traveled through villages where bosses were scourging debt-slaves who did not want to work more than eight hours a day, and all I saw were old churches and old women praying. 'Such good people,' I said to myself, not noticing that these good people were victims of cruel oppression."

The open-eyed blindness did not last long, however. The goodness of the people, which was the quality he first noted, moved him to want to know them better. Soon, when he visited a village, he would stay in the shacks of the poor. The change immediately provoked the anger of the bosses, who interpreted it correctly as undermining their traditional "rights." Attitudes developed in Spanish times, when the clergy were chosen and paid by the state, took it for granted that bishops and priests used their authority to support the rulers at all levels, including the local *caciques* ("bosses"). Don Samuel's defection to the side of the oppressed would create many problems for him. But he never hesitated.

❖

In switching sides, Don Samuel was undoubtedly influenced by his study of the sixteenth-century predecessor who had given his name to the diocese, Fray Bartolomé de Las Casas. To show his disapproval of the misdeeds of the Spaniards, Fray Bartolomé had forbidden his friars to stay or eat at their homes or to give absolution to *comenderos* (those who held indigenous as unpaid workers) or to any Spaniards unwilling to return land or goods they had robbed. The friars, he said, should stay in the huts of the indigenous; but at the same time, they should not become a burden on them by eating such expensive foods as beef or chicken.

Don Samuel's personal experience of subhuman poverty, powerlessness, and oppression on these visits, and his constant reflection in company with the pastoral agents, including the catechists, led to a radical redefining of the evangelization methods. Abandoning the traditional approach of seeking to Europeanize the indigenous, the diocese set out to incarnate the gospel in the cultures of the various communities. It was no simple task. The linguistic problem alone was a challenge. Instead of Spanish for everyone, each of five language groups had to be addressed in its own tongue. The most numerous group, the Tzeltales, live in the municipalities of Chilón, Oxchuc, and Tenejapa, all in the highlands, and in Ocosingo in the area of the Lacandon jungle. The Tzotziles live in Chamula, San Cristóbal, and Zinacantán in

the highlands, in Larraínzar in the center of the state, and
Simojovel in the north. The Chol live in Palenque and Ya-
jalón in the north; the Tojolabales, around Las Margaritas
in the southeast, near Guatemala. The Mames, one of the
biggest Mayan-Quiché families in the time of Columbus, are
found today in Soconusco and in the Pacific coastal region;
and there are also many Mam-speaking Guatemalans in the
refugee camps under the protection of the diocese since the
early 1980s. All these language groups are culturally Mayan.
They number some three-quarters of a million, 75 percent of
the entire population of the diocese.

The economy of the indigenous rests on the cultivation of
corn and the production of handicrafts. Most live in villages
or small towns. Because community in their culture ranks
before individual interests, social and political controls are
strong. This can give rise to *caciquismo* ("bossism") when
there are abuses of power or corruption. Religious expressions are partly pre-Hispanic, partly those of popular religion
that is at times influenced by Protestant fundamentalism, at
times by the post–Vatican II pastoral practices of the Catholic
Church.

A first step for the new bishop was to learn the languages,
an essential preliminary to understanding the mindset. Don
Samuel was already an outstanding linguist. In addition to a
solid command of Latin, Greek, and Hebrew, his education
had included English, French, German, and Italian. Now he
added Tzeltal and Tzotzil, the two most common languages
in the diocese, and achieved a working knowledge of Tojolabal and Chol. His associates committed themselves to learn
the language of the group with which each worked. They
took courses in anthropology and began to study indigenous
culture and religiosity. The Bible was translated into Tzeltal
and Chol, and parts of it into Tzotzil and Tojolabal.

The Jesuits and Dominicans in Chilón-Bachajón and Ocosingo, as Michael Tangeman reports in *Mexico at the Crossroads*,[10] discovered that the Tzeltal language has no word for
teacher but has a more holistic concept, "one who helps an-

other to read." They had in fact anticipated Paulo Freire's pedagogical method: learning is not a transfer of knowledge from teacher to pupil but an interaction of two people who are simultaneously teachers and learners.

The revolutionary concept was given the Tzeltal name *tijwanej* (meaning "to agitate" or "to move") and was quickly applied in catechesis. Largely through the initiative of the catechists, a catechism was put together in Tzeltal and then translated into Spanish under the title of *Estamos buscando la libertad* ("we are seeking freedom"). With its help the indigenous who had been driven by want to the Lacandon jungle were able to recognize the parallels between their experience and the slavery of the Israelites in Egypt.

By the early 1970s the number of catechists had grown into the thousands (they would be 7,800 by 1994). Catechists were not picked arbitrarily by the priest. Instead, the community selected a member judged by it to have leadership qualities, who then went to a series of courses organized by the diocese. The catechist, in consequence, started out with the support of the community and quickly became its stimulator and animator. As the people became aware both of the oppression they suffered and its mechanisms, the desire for change grew. The catechists read and interpreted the Exodus story of a people seeking liberation, explaining that God's salvific plan as revealed there called on the people of Chiapas to become agents in their own historical liberation, with a stress on the struggle for land as absolutely necessary if they were to survive as a people.

Parallel with this conscientization of the people and in dialectic relation with it was the evolution in the understanding of their role by the bishop, priests, and sisters. Don Samuel constantly proclaimed the Vatican Council's call to renewal and change. As president of CELAM's Department of Missions and the Commission for the Indigenous of the Mexican bishops, he echoed the voice of the indigenous of all Latin America, their demand that their cultural identity be recognized and respected. He praised their fidelity to their past and supported their demands of autonomy and freedom. Matching his words to his actions, he encouraged the diocese's pastoral agents to identify with the oppressed people.

The major population movements that have affected Chiapas since World War II both influenced and were influenced by this evolving diocesan strategy. By the 1960s a birthrate of 3.35 percent was putting intolerable strains on the Chiapan highlands, where the land was poor and the population density was five times the average for the entire state of Chiapas. The explosive growth brought the state population from 680,000 in 1940 to 3,210,000 in 1990.[11] Under these pressures, some of the more enterprising young people began in the 1960s to occupy Lacandona, an area of 15,000 square kilometers (6,000 square miles) in the west of Chiapas and bordering on Guatemala. Until a few years previously, when — with government encouragement — some thousands of landless peasants from states in the interior of Mexico had homesteaded here, this remote low-lying tropical jungle on the edge of the Chiapan highlands had been uninhabited since the time of the Spanish colonization except for a few thousand Lacandon-speaking indigenous. Many of the first arrivals from the highlands of Chiapas were Protestants who had decided to move from the hostile environment of Chamula, a major municipality not far from San Cristóbal, which — as discussed in detail later — was then and still is dominated by caciques ("bosses"). Inspired by their religious convictions, they formed "cities of God" as suggested by St. Augustine, giving them such biblical names as Jerusalén, Jericó, Betania. They had fled to avoid conflicts they judged useless, but the conflicts came with them. In early 1994 they were strafed by Mexican air force planes sent to attack the Zapatistas.

As word spread that land was available simply by squatting and cutting down the jungle, indigenous of all the major language groups joined the pioneers. They had many reasons for coming. Some were tired of working as day laborers for nominal wages. Others were escaping from the *enganchadores* ("hiring agents," literally "hookers") who had given them an advance and would jail them for failure to repay. Others again were Protestants who were being expelled from communities, especially Chamula, in which they challenged the control of the *caciques*. Their mood was expressed by the names they gave their villages: *El Triunfo* ("triumph"), *La Esperanza* ("hope"), *El Porvenir* ("the future").

Each new colony formed a committee to create an *ejido*. The *ejido* is the traditional form of landholding of the indigenous Mexicans, and its legalization was one of the principal goals of the 1910 Revolution. Article 27 of the 1917 Constitution provided that any group of twenty or more citizens could claim, at no cost, contiguous plots of land held by the state or by large private landowners, on condition they themselves worked this land.[12] Each member could pass his title to his descendants but had no right to mortgage or sell his share. Many of the committees succeeded in obtaining a "presidential resolution," an administrative recognition of their claim. But the ownership documents were executed in only a few cases, so that most of the squatters were never given legal title.

Religion has played an important part in the evolution of the Lacandon communities. Already in the 1940s, the Mexican government encouraged the activities of Protestant missionaries associated with the U.S.-based Summer Institute of Linguistics. The government's interest was in the insertion of the indigenous population of Lacandona, then quite small, into the mestizo culture of the country. The Summer Institute missionaries discouraged traditional cultural practices and promoted the incorporation of the indigenous into the market economy by the introduction of new cash crops, all objectives sought by the state.

It was not long until the new colonists found themselves in conflict with the timber companies, many of them foreign-owned, that had been exploiting the region's hardwoods since the late nineteenth century. The largest rain forest in North

America, it contains 40 percent of Mexico's plant varieties, 36 percent of its mammals, 34 percent of its reptiles and amphibians, 66 percent of its birds, and 20 percent of its freshwater fish. Commercial exploitation of its hardwoods and the domestic use of firewood have combined in the last thirty years to destroy 70 percent of its trees, a destruction rate even higher than that of the forests of the Amazon.

Although the federal government had initially encouraged the colonization of Lacandona as a way to ease the pressure of the peasants for land, it quickly succumbed to the pressures of the big timber companies, which saw the colonists as threatening their control of the forest. During the presidency of Luis Echeverría (1960–66), the government suddenly discovered that the jungle belonged to the Lacandon tribe and issued a presidential decree restoring their rights. At that time, there were sixty families of Lacandons in the region and about six thousand families of migrants from the Chiapan highlands. Although historians had determined that there was no continuity between the historical inhabitants of Lacandona and these sixty families, the government gave them title to 614,300 hectares, more than a million and a half acres. The six thousand migrant families were declared trespassers and ordered to move to a small area where they were promised land titles, public services, and infrastructure.

The object of this exercise became apparent when the Lacandons, just as soon as their title had been certified, signed a ten-year contract with the timber companies, authorizing them to extract ten thousand mahogany and cedar trees a year.

The failure of the government to fulfil its commitments to the few communities that moved to the area allotted to them gave an enormous impetus to the politicization of the jungle colonists. In the 1970s and 1980s, they formed a vast array of organizations, developed techniques to defend themselves from attempts to expel them, and organized brigades to retake land from which they had been driven. They played a major part in the 1974 Indigenous Congress (see below), and the Zapatista uprising followed naturally from the failure of the government to respond.[13]

❖

Don Samuel had not been slow to recognize the need to extend the services of the diocese to this new frontier. He visited the various communities and encouraged them to select some of their young people to train as catechists. These were then delegated with powers normally reserved to priests, a further step in the indigenization and democratization of the diocese. The approach of the priests and catechists was very different from that of the Protestant missionaries. They sought to rescue the indigenous traditions and practices, while promoting cooperatives as highly compatible with the community-oriented culture of the people.

Sharing with their communities the liberation theology exegesis of the Exodus story as the people's struggle from slavery to liberation, the catechists began to transfer the democratic and cultural habits they were acquiring in the church to the new civil society the people were building. It was the perfect social and cultural context for the slow nurturing of what became the Zapatista movement. The state authorities, understandably unhappy with these developments, continued to channel social benefits to the Protestant communities in the hope of limiting the influence of the priests and catechists. They did exacerbate differences, but a surprising revelation of the Zapatista uprising was the high level of Protestant support and participation.

Parallel with the commitment of the diocese to accompany the people in their search for integral liberation, the popular movement developed, and peasant organizations proliferated. A key moment was the "Fray Bartolomé de Las Casas" Congress of the Indigenous in San Cristóbal in January 1974, co-sponsored by the diocese and the public authorities.

The initiative for the congress came from Chiapas state Governor Manuel Velasco Suárez in 1971. Recognizing that his credibility vis-à-vis the indigenous communities was

rapidly evaporating, he decided to put on a public relations
performance to relax tensions: a commemoration of the fifth
centenary of the birth, in 1474, of Fray Bartolomé de Las
Casas. Aware, however, that a direct approach would simply
be rebuffed, he turned to the bishop of San Cristóbal to take
the initiative in convoking the celebration.

The state authorities discovered too late that they had
made a serious mistake in enlisting Don Samuel as convener.
He immediately set out to organize community-level groups
in all parts of the diocese. In these groups, the people elaborated their specific complaints, demands, and proposals. He
also invited students and professors to help catechists in providing courses in agrarian law, economics, agronomy, and the
history of Mexico.

The process resulted in a substantial advance in the self-
identity and organizational structures of the indigenous, and
it developed a new generation of indigenous community leaders highly conscientized about the causes of poverty and
injustice.

A thousand communities representing four hundred thousand people became actively involved in the preparations.
They collected the experience of the new communities in
the Lacandon jungle and shared it with the older communities in the highlands. They gathered protests and defined
problems, focusing on the issues of land tenure, commerce,
education, and health. These four themes anticipated the
points (work, land, shelter, nutrition, health, education, independence, liberty, democracy, justice, and peace) of the
proclamation issued by the Zapatistas when they rose in arms
on New Year's Day 1994.

The declared purpose of the congress, as formulated by the
bishop, was to let the indigenous speak, and for three days
they did just that. They chose as presenters "men and women
of good words," by which they meant people they could trust
to match words and actions. Except for the opening address
of welcome in Spanish by the governor, the proceedings were
conducted exclusively in four indigenous languages, young

interpreters from multiethnic communities around Las Margaritas and Comitán doing the translations, and the people spoke with unprecedented frankness. Drawn from 327 communities, the delegates included 587 Tzeltales, 350 Tzotziles, 152 Tojolabales, and 161 Choles.[14] They proclaimed the right of the indigenous to land, education, and health, to adequate transport from farm to market, to the opportunity to get the benefit of their labor by the creation of facilities to process and commercialize their products. Specifically, they demanded an end to land evictions and to the timber concessions that had been granted to U.S. and Mexican companies in the Lacandon jungle, and they claimed the right to organize their own cooperatives.

They also told the church what they expected from it: a catechesis that would encourage the recovery of and respect for the people's historical memory, its ministries, symbols, and values, and specifically the development of an indigenous clergy.

Far from performing the function intended by the state authorities, the process brought about a substantial advance in the self-identity, militancy, and organizational structures of the indigenous. It also developed a new generation of indigenous community leaders highly conscientized about the structural causes of poverty and injustice.

While the Indigenous Congress was in session in San Cristóbal, dissidents occupied the municipal buildings of Chamula, protesting the expulsion from the municipality of all who opposed the exactions of the *caciques*. They were supported by students from the teacher training college in Tuxtla Gutiérrez, the capital of Chiapas, in a rare demonstration of mestizo support for an indigenous protest. It was the first impact of the Lacandon jungle on the thinking of the Chiapan highlands.

The response of the power structures, disappointed by their failure to manipulate the proceedings, was iron-handed. Ten days after the congress closed, the state authorities, who depended on the *caciques* to deliver the vote at election times,

arrested 230 people in Chamula and expelled them from the
municipality. A little later the army occupied five villages in
the Lacandon jungle and burned the houses. It was a fore-
taste of the official response to the decision of the people to
assume responsibility for their lives.

"When we pastoral agents of the diocese saw and heard
how the indigenous described their situation," Don Samuel
wrote later about the congress, "it became very clear that
our pastoral plan had been drawn up without taking into account the aspirations, needs, and hopes of the communities.
We began again."[15]

*Chapter 2*

# THE DIOCESAN
# PASTORAL PLAN

N O HASTY attempt at a face-saving adjustment, the new
beginning involved a radical restructuring of the entire
process of evangelization. It started with the See-Judge-Act
evaluation approach developed by Canon (later Cardinal)
Cardijn of Belgium in the Young Christian Worker movement, an approach adopted in its deliberations by the Second
Vatican Council and subsequently by liberation theology. The
results are formulated in a diocesan plan approved at a general diocesan assembly in August 1986. It is a document
that many believe can be offered as a model for all church
workers engaged in evangelization of peoples belonging to
a culture other than European and to a mindset other than
Aristotelian.

The plan opens with an affirmation of the principle spelled
out by the Vatican Council that the seeds of the word are already present in the many religions practiced by people who
have never heard of Christ. The first duty of the evangelizer
is "to discover the riches that the Father gave to his children
even before our humble proclamation of the Good News."
The task, consequently, is not to denounce and eliminate existing beliefs, but to build on them to bring those who profess
them to a full understanding of the Christian message. In addition, we have to recognize that members of other faiths

and even non-believers are our brothers and sisters, and that we must welcome their contribution to the extent that they devote themselves to building the Kingdom or community of God.

This position is today generally accepted at the conceptual level. There is, nevertheless, widespread resistance to implementing it. Latin American religious educators, in particular, have to overcome serious psychological obstacles because it asks them to repudiate the methods used from the outset to impose Christianity on the region: the physical destruction of temples and holy places as well as of amulets and other objects of devotion. The general public has similarly to surmount emotional and social barriers, because it elevates the indigenous to equality with those who took pride in their possession of the Good News, rejecting the rationale by which the latter justified their wealth in the midst of poverty. No wonder that the power brokers and power holders of Chiapas want to get rid of the bishop of San Cristóbal!

❖

After the opening statement of purpose, the plan devotes a long section to an analysis of the social, economic, and political conditions and trends in the diocese, the context in which the diocese carries out its mission. This concentration on the objective reality of daily life is one of the distinguishing marks of the work of Don Samuel.

The assembly, at which the plan was adopted, fully understood the reason for this focus. "Let our diocesan assembly," it declared, "in union with the Latin American church, proclaim the practice of Jesus and live it in participative and fraternal community, committing itself and serving the people, inserting itself as Jesus did in the process of liberation of the oppressed in which they may be the agents of history, so that together we may build the new society as an anticipation of the Kingdom."[16]

One thing comes through very clearly from the analysis. The indigenous of Chiapas are not living in a sleepy backwater in which nothing ever changes, as might appear to the tourist or other casual outside observer to be the case. This is a world in ferment and the rapid changes are mostly not good news for the people who live there. The evaluation made at the 1986 assembly showed how rapidly things were deteriorating. The following years accelerated the negative trends.

Two new sources of wealth had been generated in the twenty years before the congress, petroleum and hydroelectricity. The three contiguous states of Tabasco, Campeche, and Chiapas produce 80 percent of Mexico's oil and gas, the share of Chiapas being a third of the gas and nearly a quarter of the petroleum. Thanks to heavy rainfall, which in places reaches 5,000 mm (200 inches) annually, the state's hydroelectric potential is even greater than that of its hydrocarbon fuels. The portion already utilized accounts for 60 percent of Mexico's hydroelectric production. Some of it is exported to the United States and to Belize, yet 35 percent of Chiapan homes — and a much higher proportion in the highlands where the power is generated — have no electricity.

All of this wealth, moreover, is inequitably distributed. Big landowners and businessmen are the main beneficiaries within the state. But even they have to pay an enormous tribute to the transnational corporations and the international banking system. Foreign banks, the diocesan assembly report estimated, take 70 percent of Mexico's revenue from petroleum to service the external debt. Maldistribution within the state is illustrated by wage differentials. Workers in industry and in the energy sector, in both of which few indigenous are employed, earn ten times as much and thirty-one times as much, respectively, as do agricultural laborers. These wage differentials are understandably reflected in the indices of the quality of life in the state. Eighty percent of homes have dirt floors; 80 percent have no potable water supply; 60 percent have no drainage; 72 percent of school-goers don't finish the first grade; 50 percent of schools have only one teacher; fifty thousand die each year — as the first Zapatista communiqué in January 1994 reminded the world — of easily curable diseases.

This unjust situation understandably causes popular discontent that expresses itself in many ways, some of them negative or counterproductive. These range from criticism of the government to rejection of the labor union controlled by the PRI, land takeovers, killing of landowners, protest marches and meetings, organization of unions of *ejidos*, even creative infiltration of the official party (PRI).

Various ideologies seek to explain the problems and propose solutions. Some are motivated by traditional religion, by apparitions and talking stones. They may believe in a new messiah or in millenarian catastrophes. Others look to liberation theology to guide them. Yet others advocate various forms of Marxism, some of these insisting that only armed struggle can provide a solution. According to the analysis presented in the diocesan plan, the expansion of religious sects and the invasion of investigators and anthropologists have a greater impact and are more significant than is generally realized. The reason offered is that in some cases the outsiders manipulate the thinking of the indigenous so that they adopt a neutral stance toward the class struggle and Marxism; in other cases, they weaken their sense of nationalism and persuade people to reject liberation theology.[17]

On the basis of this in-depth analysis of the lived reality, the plan sets out a program of action for the pastoral workers and all the people. A first step is to advance the democratization of the diocese by creating, both in the cities and in the countryside, base communities that will share resources, power, and knowledge. Liturgical expressions in which the people can celebrate their struggles, successes, and failures are to be encouraged. In this way the gospel is incarnated in the community, making it possible to hope for and advance toward liberation.

For the pastoral workers the praxis of Jesus must constitute the foundation of their liberating work. They must learn from the people, letting themselves be evangelized by the people. In proclaiming the Word of God, they should confront their existential situation in such a way as to bring about a synthesis between faith and politics. Liturgical actions and expressions of popular religiosity should be directed to the furtherance of change. Theological reflection should accompany pastoral action. The liberating aspects of popular religiosity should be encouraged. Not only the pastoral agents but the people as a whole should inform themselves about the oppressive system and its mechanisms. Workshops and courses should be held to help this systemic analysis. Women should participate in decision-making on a basis of total equality.

❖

Another major initiative of the diocese in the carrying out of its stated purposes was the creation in March 1989 of the Fray Bartolomé de Las Casas Human Rights Center. The need for such a center had been demonstrated by a 1986 Amnesty International report that documented the archaic and barbaric mechanisms employed in the oppression of both indigenous and mestizo campesinos. State and federal authorities quickly recognized that the center was one more challenge to their repressive practices, as indeed it was. The first issue of the center's bulletin demonstrated the need for such a watchdog. Assembling only materials available on the public record, it listed 4,732 cases of repressive actions between January 1974 and July 1987 to which public authority was a party: assassinations, tortures, imprisonments, theft of titles to land, repression of protest marches.

From its creation, the center worked in close cooperation with other church-supported human rights organizations. The most important of these were the Jesuit-sponsored Miguel A. Pro Juárez Human Rights Center, the Commission in Solidarity and Defense of Human Rights located in the chancery of the diocese of Chihuahua and headed by Jesuit Bishop Llaguno, and the Dominican order's Fray Francisco Vitoria Human Rights Center.

The San Cristóbal center quickly became an important channel for marshalling public opinion when official agencies of government violated the rights of the indigenous or of the peasants of Chiapas. Presenting a report at the Center for Theological Reflection in Mexico City on human rights violations during the previous five months, Don Samuel said in September 1991 that the state government of Chiapas, groups connected to the big landowners, the alcohol vendors, and the judicial authorities were responsible for a "disturbing growth of repression." New elements of conflict, he added, were being introduced by the process of regional economic integration to which the national government was committed. Examples of human rights violations cited included the "arbitrary and violent" detention by the state police of 129 members of the Union of *Ejiditarios* who were on their way in trucks to Mexico City to seek redress from the president. The eighteen women and four children in the group, the bishop said, were brutally beaten, the women stripped naked.

Not surprisingly, the charges got major attention in the media. Miguel Concha Malo, O.P., a theologian with an international reputation, director of the Fray Vitoria Human Rights Center, and a columnist in a major Mexico City newspaper, wrote: "Arbitrary arrests, tortures, expulsions and removals of peasants, physical attacks, illegal or arbitrary deprivation of liberty, extortions. Just to list these violations of human rights gives a slight indication of the climate that prevails in Chiapas."[18]

In his Christmas 1993 pastoral letter, the bishop responded to criticisms that he was improperly appealing to public opinion outside the diocese. This, he insisted, was the only weapon he had to denounce the "brutal suppression of civil protests, the still unresolved problems of expulsions of both Catholics and Protestants from Chamula, expulsions now continuing for twenty years, and — above all — torture inflicted by some members of the armed forces and other official agencies."[19]

Confirmation for the bishop's charges came in the Amnesty

International report for 1993. Mexico, it said, has one of the worst records in the world as a violator of human rights. And within Mexico, Chiapas is one of the worst states. "The forces of order, both state and federal, continue to engage in torture, repression, coercion, injustice, extra-judicial executions, and death threats." In June, for example, the Judicial Police raided Chalam del Carmen and four neighboring villages, destroying a dozen homes and beating men, women, and children randomly. Twenty-three persons, including two minors and three old people — 80, 90, and 102 years old — were arrested, tortured and imprisoned. In jail they were tortured, for three days. They were beaten, half smothered with alcohol inserted in their noses, given electric shocks, and forced to sign confessions in Spanish, a language none of them knew. The 102-year-old, released after eighteen days, was hospitalized for the beatings he had received. Ten were still held at year end. "No action was taken to investigate the charges of torture."

# Chapter 3

# CONFLICT WITH
# CIVIL AUTHORITY

ㅤ

Eᴀʀʟʏ in his pastoral activity, Dom Samuel had alien-
ated powerful individuals by abandoning the tradition
of living in the homes of the rich when traveling around the
diocese. As he identified progressively with the indigenous
and supported their efforts to become subjects of their own
destiny, he accumulated more enemies. To understand the dy-
namics of this conflict, it is necessary to review the history of
racism and its concrete expressions in Chiapas.

The racial hierarchy established by the conquerors placed
those born in Spain on top, the *criollos* ("creoles," American-
born descendants of Spaniards) next, followed by mestizos or
*ladinos* (offspring of Spanish fathers and indigenous moth-
ers), and at the bottom the indigenous, the pre-invasion
inhabitants who retained the languages and cultural traits of
their ancestors.

With independence in the first quarter of the nineteenth
century the Spaniards were eliminated as a social force,
leaving the *criollos* as the ruling class. In the twentieth century, the mestizos have developed into a middle class with
substantial political power.

The boundaries of Guatemala established at the moment
of independence included Chiapas. In 1834, however, a pleb-
iscite — in which only *criollos* and mestizos had votes —
transferred the political control to Mexico. Culturally, never-

theless, Chiapas remained — and to a large extent still remains — part of Guatemala. Even after it was annexed by Mexico, little effort was made to integrate it into the national economy. There was no direct road to Mexico City until the Pan-American highway reached San Cristóbal in 1944.

Now there always has been an important difference in the way in which the *criollos* and mestizos in Mexico and those in Guatemala view the indigenous, whom they call Indians, a misnomer resulting from the mistaken belief of the Spaniards that the land they had run into in the Ocean Sea was India. The Mexican myth is schizophrenic. It accords the "Indians" a key role in the construction of the state. It honors them, however, only when they are dead. Those now alive are denied a part in society in every possible way. As novelist and social critic Carlos Fuentes has put it: "We have always congratulated ourselves in Mexico on our extraordinary Indian culture, which we display in museums and through imposing monuments along our boulevards.... In actual practice, however, we have treated the Indians with more cruelty, perhaps, than Cortés did."[20] This means that the national model consists of a glorious "Indian" past that has been absorbed into a homogeneous mestizo present.

The Guatemalan ideology or myth is significantly different and more straightforward. There, the people who are biologically mestizo imagine that they are *criollos*. In spite of the visible racial identity, they insist that the Spaniards are their only ancestors. They call themselves *ladinos* ("latins") and "the people of reason." The indigenous are by definition people without reason. They are not entitled to have any opinions. They are thought of and treated as animals. Indeed it is a common complaint of the indigenous that they are treated worse than animals. A sign that hung for years in the Lion's Club in Ocosingo sums up the common attitude of the ruling class in Chiapas: "The law of the jungle says that you kill grackles and Indians." In the same spirit, Patricio González Garrido, when governor of Chiapas (1988–93), referred to the indigenous as FBI (*fuerza bruta indígena*).[21]

In this regard, as in many others, Chiapas follows Guatemala. Denying that they are racially mixed, the *ladinos* of Chiapas organize society racially, relegating the indigenous to the margins. An example of their intolerance is a city ordinance passed by San Cristóbal in 1909 that prohibited the indigenous from walking through the central park at any time and from walking in the city streets at night, and that ordered them to step off the footpath to allow "the people of reason" to pass. It was not until the 1930s, during the presidency of Emiliano Zapata, that the ordinance was rescinded. Not without reason have the armed indigenous in the Lacandon jungle called their movement the Zapatista Army of National Liberation (EZLN).

❖

Underlying the disdain for the indigenous is a fear that is unacknowledged at the conscious level. After all, this was their country, and why should they not want to repossess it? As Mexican anthropologist Martha Turok (who lives in San Cristóbal) describes it, "The civilized don't want the uncivilized to develop, because they fear the unknown. They say they are a risk factor; they might ask for autonomy and then they are going to destroy the nation."[22] Indigenous autonomy was indeed one of the demands formulated by the Zapatistas on New Year's Day 1994.

In 1849, fifteen years after it annexed Chiapas, Mexico enacted a law prohibiting forced and uncompensated labor. The Chiapan landowners, outraged at this subversion of their established order, rose in revolt. Within two years, the Mexican government gave in and rescinded the law. Even when the Revolution of 1910 succeeded in eliminating debt peonage in the rest of the country, it hung on in Chiapas.

Attempts in 1914 to extend land reform to Chiapas brought another rebellion and a threat to secede to Guatemala. Again the central government yielded. Not only did it agree not to expropriate private property, as it was doing elsewhere, but it handed over control of the state to the *Fa-*

*milia Chiapaneca,* the handful of local *criollos* who have ever since monopolized power. When the curiously named Party of the Institutionalized Revolution (PRI) came to power in 1928, it confirmed the autonomy of the *Familia Chiapaneca* in return for delivering a 100 percent *ladino* and indigenous vote for PRI in federal elections. How effective this arrangement proved to be is evidenced by the results of the 1991 congressional elections, in which Chiapas had more municipalities that voted 100 percent PRI than any other state. So well oiled was the machine that in San Juan Cancuc 102 percent of the inhabitants were registered to vote.[23] The other side of the deal was that the PRI has never established in Chiapas its own political structures to the same extent as elsewhere, thus remaining dependent on support of the *Familia Chiapaneca* to retain its monopoly of power at the national level.

The extreme hostility that Don Samuel has provoked within the oligarchy of Chiapas can be understood only within this historical context. To tell the indigenous that they are intelligent human beings from whom the rest of us can learn is treason. To assert that they are the church and call on them to evangelize the rest of us is blasphemy. It undermines the established order and threatens the monopoly of power. Given that mentality, one can understand how solid citizens and regular church-goers can demonstrate in front of a church and denounce their bishop as a communist and the Antichrist.

The commitment to get rid of this troublesome cleric has grown since it became evident in the early 1980s that the conscientization of the indigenous promoted by Don Samuel and his thousands of pastoral workers was in fact developing a hitherto unknown combativeness. For his part, the bishop has never backed off from the conflict. As he gradually recognized the structural roots of the misery of Chiapas, he steadily moved the defense of the indigenous to the national and international level, determined to use every available means to assert their rights.

Several factors converged during the 1980s to promote the conscientization of the indigenous and their determination to improve their condition. An economic crisis in 1982 increased unemployment. Its empty spaces already fully occupied, the Lacandon jungle was no longer an escape valve for surplus workers. An influx of Guatemalans fleeing for their lives, who provided an even cheaper labor force for landowners, further aggravated unemployment. Converts to Protestantism and other objectors to the control of the *caciques* in the villages, for whom Lacandona had for a time provided asylum, now flocked to the cities. San Cristóbal, hitherto inhabited almost exclusively by *ladinos* and controlled by *criollos* (who call themselves *coletos* — the pigtailed ones) expanded until more than a third of its population was Tzotzil and Tzeltal. The newcomers live in some fifty shanty towns, with no employment base. From being rural landless, they have become urban workless.

There are differences, however. With their aroused consciousness, they have become more creative. They develop their own organizations that bypass political programs and work on day-to-day problems of the communities. Protestants of many denominations, whose leaders were formed in the ecumenical climate of the Lacandon jungle, work with Catholics and with the opposition political parties, the rightist PAN (Party of National Action) and the leftist PRD (Democratic Republican Party).

The Protestants even began to accumulate arms after the *caciques* of Chamula in 1991 sent an armed band to attack a squatter village, the Colonia La Hormiga, in San Cristóbal. A leader of the Adventist settlement of Getsemani jailed in Cerro Hueco organized a hunger strike of the prisoners and succeeded in having ninety-two released. Protestants expelled from Betania seized two members of the dreaded judicial police. Various communities guarded and fed the prisoners for three weeks while the governor of Chiapas, Patrocinio González Garrido, negotiated for their release, committing himself to reforms that were never implemented.

❖

Violations of human rights in Chiapas again attracted national attention when four hundred indigenous set out on
foot from Palenque, March 7, 1992, to reach Mexico City six
weeks later. The protest was provoked by the violent disper-
sal by the state police of members of the Committee for the
Defense of Indigenous Liberty who had assembled in Palenque in December 1991. They had met to protest corruption of
municipal presidents, the imposition by the municipal authorities of village officials, and the constitutional changes that
threatened the survival of the *ejido* system of land tenure. Ap-
plying a clause introduced into the state penal code in 1989
that classified unarmed mass protests "by the mentally weak,
minors, or illiterate people who do not speak Spanish" as a
threat to public order punishable with up to four years' imprisonment, the police arrested more than a hundred people
and beat and tortured several of them.

In Mexico City the marchers gained promises of redress
from federal officials, but as usual no significant action en-
sued. The state penal code was not reformed, no police were
brought to trial, and municipal presidents continued to name
their cronies as village officials. And, needless to say, the constitutional changes affecting the *ejido* were maintained. But
there was one important result. An organization formed in
the Lacandon jungle and the highlands in 1989 changed its
name to the Emiliano Zapata National Independent Campesino Alliance (ANCIEZ) and announced that it had a base in
six states.

So rapid was the growth of ANCIEZ that half of the ten
thousand indigenous who converged on San Cristóbal on
October 12, 1992, the fifth centenary of the Spanish invasion, were its members. Joining with demonstrators of all
creeds and many organizations, they took over the streets and
plazas of the city and smashed the statue of the Conquistador
who had founded it (with the name of Ciudad Real), Diego
de Mazariegos.[24] Three months later the indigenous commu-

nity of Chilalhó organized a march that led to the freeing of several prisoners.

These disturbances occurred while the Latin American bishops were holding the fourth CELAM Conference in Santo Domingo. Shortly after that conference ended, Don Samuel joined three other bishops of Mexico's Southern Pacific region, Bartolomé Carrasco, Arturo Lona Reyes, and Hermenegildo Ramírez, in a statement supportive of the demands of the rioters. Citing the Santo Domingo document, they called on the Mexican church "to recognize the original peoples of America."

The protests in the highlands were shortly followed by the erection of roadblocks in the Lacandon jungle to obstruct the trucks of the timber merchants. What this meant was that the indigenous of the highlands were coordinating their protests with the Zapatistas who had for years been assembling and training an army in Lacandona. And in fact the latter in March 1993 carried out their first guerrilla operation. As Subcomandante Marcos later reported, it was brought off by a unit composed entirely of women, most of them Tzotziles, and without a single casualty. Using U.S. helicopter gunships, the Mexican armed forces took their revenge in January 1994 for this affront. In response to the Zapatista uprising, they strafed several shanty towns on the outskirts of San Cristóbal.

That same month of March 1993 saw a major clash between Don Samuel and the military commander of Chiapas. The bishop publicly protested as illegal the seizure and torture of Tzotzil villagers suspected of having been involved in the killing of two army officers. When the bishop succeeded in having the villagers freed, the commander publicly accused him of impeding justice and insulting the army. In Mexico to insult the army is a crime carrying heavy penalties.

As governor of Chiapas and later as secretary of the interior in the federal government (where he would become a political casualty of the Zapatista uprising), Patrocinio González Garrido was an inveterate enemy of Don Samuel.

He correctly identified the bishop as the greatest challenge to the structural changes to which, in cooperation with President Salinas de Gortari, he was committed. A declared anticleric and heir to one of the biggest fortunes in the *Familia Chiapaneca*, González is a cousin by marriage of Salinas. The grandiose Salinas project, regarded by Mexico's power brokers as essential to the success of the neoliberal North American Free Trade Agreement (NAFTA), called for nothing less than the elimination of the indigenous — the overwhelming majority of the inhabitants of the diocese of San Cristóbal — as a social force. If successful, it will render them economically superfluous and condemn them to administrative genocide.

The "free market" ideology underlying NAFTA required, among other things, the ending of the *ejido* system of landholding that was a major achievement of the Mexican Revolution of 1910. The objective was accomplished, as already noted, by amending Article 27 of the Constitution.

The impact of the constitutional amendment was far greater in Chiapas than in any other part of Mexico, because the land reform mandated by the 1917 Constitution had been only minimally implemented in Chiapas. Political resistance to redistribution of land had begun as far back as 1914. Ranchers and estate owners organized a successful counter-revolution in the following years. In 1920, one of their leaders, Tiburcio Fernández Ruiz, became governor, and he decreed that individual private owners could hold up to 8,000 hectares (20,000 acres). With few exceptions, land reform in Chiapas involved the colonization of publicly owned and unused forestal areas in the Lacandon jungle. And few of those who had been allowed to settle in the jungle succeeded in getting the titles that would guarantee their ownership of their *ejidos*.

Salinas paid a heavy political price for the structural reforms he pushed through. It was his abandonment of one of the primary goals of the 1910 Revolution, said Subcomandante Marcos in his first communiqué in January

1994, that provoked the Zapatista uprising. Article 27, combined with cut-backs in credits and subsidies to small farmers (also required as part of the "structural adjustment" program), will leave most *ejiditarios* with no choice but to sell to cattle ranchers or to the multinationals interested in growing luxury crops for export. Studies by the Mexican Secretariat for Agriculture estimate that up to a million farm families in the south of the country will be eliminated by massive imports of corn. The result will be an increase in the already substantial population movement north toward and across the border with the United States.

❖

The modernization program to which the incoming Salinas presidency committed itself in 1988 was governed by macro-economic concepts unrelated to the reality of peasant life. They bore particularly harshly on Chiapas, a state in which in 1990 agriculture constituted nearly 60 percent of all economic activity. They meant an almost complete absence of new investment in the countryside, a drying up of credit, and markets saturated with imported grains. Of the foreign investment that flowed to Mexico with the inauguration of NAFTA less than 1 percent went into agriculture. With reason the Zapatistas described NAFTA as "a death certificate for the indigenous people."

Chiapas is a very rich state, not only potentially but actually. It produces half of the coffee that in 1984 was Mexico's second biggest source of foreign exchange. For the indigenous and peasants, coffee constituted up to a decade ago a major source of money income, a source over which they have no control because the price of coffee is dictated by world economic forces. In addition, the price of coffee, as of other primary products, constantly declines in relation to the cost of manufactured products the producers of these commodities have to buy. The collapse of the International Coffee Agreement in 1989 created a crisis. Instead of moving to support producers, the Salinas government introduced a series of institutional reforms dictated by the World Bank. Before it would disburse further structural loans, the bank insisted on a radical overhaul of the agricultural sector, including the privatization of state-owned enterprises and the gradual elimination of price supports and other input subsidies. An immediate casualty was the state agency that had been purchasing and marketing coffee, leaving the small producers at the mercy of middlemen. In the following five years, the income of small coffee producers suffered a 70 percent decline. Caught in a cycle of debt and poverty, unable to get new loans because they could not repay the old ones, thousands of small producers were simply forced to abandon coffee production.

The 1989 institutional reforms affected far more than the producers of coffee. They represented a process of transition to the free market economy that ignored the impact on all small farmers. Their interests were being subordinated to the macroeconomic goals of the Salinas administration: the use of wage and price controls to hold inflation down, privatization of state enterprises, and trade liberalization.

Chiapas is also Mexico's biggest producer of corn, with 1.2 million tons in 1984, of which more than a quarter was sold outside the state. Its price was already then threatened by cheap imports. Disparities in capitalization, technological development, subsidies, infrastructure, and climate mean that Chiapas corn growers will be unable to compete with those of the United States under the rules established by the NAFTA treaty. With its coming into force on New Year's Day 1994, the system of licenses and tariffs that previously governed the importation of corn from the United States into Mexico was replaced by a tariff-free quota and a variable tariff on imports above the quota for fifteen years, after which all corn imports would be tariff-free. The tariff-free quota was fixed at 2.5 million tons for 1994, the quota to grow at a 3 percent annual compounded rate over a fifteen-year transition period. The over-quota tariff would be similarly phased out by annual reductions over the same period.

The implementation of the structural adjustment program quickly widened the gap in Mexico between a few rich and the more than half the citizens who live below the poverty line. Between 1991 and 1994 alone, the number of billionaires (U.S. dollars) grew from three to twenty-four. One of them is Carlos Slim Helu, with net assets of $6.6 billion. Another, Carlos Cabal Peniche, who made his entire fortune during the Salinas presidency, is under investigation by the Mexican authorities for illegal lending practices and by the U.S. Drug Enforcement Administration for suspected links to a Colombian drug cartel. The concentration of wealth by 1993 was such that twenty-four families had a net worth of $44 billion, equivalent to a third of the national debt.[25]

These were the years during which, as a result of decreased spending on social services, Mexico fell from forty-fifth to fifty-third place on the Human Development Index of the United Nations. In 1994, all the rest of Latin America had only eighteen billionaires. Mexico is now outnumbered in the number of its billionaires by only the three wealthiest and most highly industrialized countries in the world, the United States, Germany, and Japan.

Chiapas was always the stepchild of the Mexican economy, and its continued and growing marginalization was guaranteed by the policy, adopted by the Mexican government in the 1970s and brought to completion by NAFTA, of incorporating it into capitalist development. The role ascribed to it was and is to provide agricultural, forest, and mineral raw materials to be processed elsewhere. The most fertile areas are singled out for intensive production involving high capitalization and consequently benefiting only large-scale operations, mostly transnational corporations. Soconusco and the Valle de Cintalapa near the Pacific coast, for example, will raise beef cattle to be shipped north as yearlings for fattening in San Luis Potosí, Hidalgo, and Veracruz, and ultimate export to the United States. To support this quality cattle enterprise, other areas are being shifted from corn and beans to peanuts, marañon, sorghum, and sunflower, crops that yield both oil and cattle feed. Highly capitalized, they are accessible only to the wealthy, and they require far less labor than traditional subsistence crops. A tobacco company is subsidizing *ejiditarios* in Soconusco to grow tobacco.

Another major project for Chiapas is the Ruta Maya ("road of the Maya"), a development of commercial tourism from Tuxtla Gutiérrez through San Cristóbal to the Mayan center of Palenque, to include luxury hotels and restaurants and to be financed with private, state, federal, and World Bank money. All the indigenous will get out of this is some low-paying jobs, far fewer than they lose in the economic rationalization. Transnationals export the profits.

❖

When Patrocinio González Garrido was chosen in 1988 by the national PRI as governor of Chiapas and "modernizer," he was faced with a number of enemies. He had to deal with the traditional cattlemen, with their private armies, opposed to change and in particular to interference from official agencies. Avoiding direct confrontation, he used the growing combativeness of the peasant organizations that were demanding land, credits, and cancellation of debts to weaken the cattle ranchers. When peasants squatted on ranch land, instead of sending the army to expel them, he called for negotiations and urged the ranchers to sell. Many of them in fact did. By contrast, attempts by campesinos to occupy the modern cattle enterprises on the coast were ruthlessly suppressed by the army.

While González sought in some instances, especially when it favored his policy of weakening the power of the ranchers, to ease the militancy of the peasants by giving them some land, his general policy was repression. During his time as governor he enacted laws that, combined with the venality of the judicial system in enforcing them, left Chiapas with the most repressive and anti-democratic system in all Mexico. Nor did he make any attempt to eliminate the private armies of the ranchers, judging them to be powerful allies against the growing peasant militancy.

He correctly judged, however, that the biggest obstacle to his goal of restructuring Chiapas to make the indigenous population economically superfluous and effectively eliminate them as a social force was Don Samuel's pastoral policy. He was determined to get rid of him, and though a self-declared anti-clerical, he turned to high church officials to help him.

*Chapter 4*

# RIFTS IN
# THE MEXICAN CHURCH

L IKE MANY other Latin American countries, Mexico has
had a long history of church-state conflict. A branch of
government in Spanish times, the institutional church was
part of a repressive system and resistant to change. The Inquisition was widely used to censor dissident ideas and punish
those who disseminated them.

The thought of the eighteenth-century Enlightenment,
however, with its glorification of the individual and its
assertion of liberty and equality, could not be eternally excluded. Its vector in Latin America was Freemasonry, which
won wide support among business sectors resentful of the
church's power and wealth. The church acquired additional
enemies during the struggle for emancipation from Spain in
the nineteenth century. Both Rome and the bishops — all
Spanish-born — sided with Spain. For many years there was
an impasse while Rome refused to recognize the independence of the former Spanish possessions or to name bishops
to dioceses that became vacant.

The political society that emerged in the new nations reflected this conflict. Two parties, Conservative and Liberal,
long dominated public life everywhere. In some countries —
especially Colombia — they still do. The Conservatives were
identified with the church, big landowners, and reaction;

the Liberals, with Freemasonry, business, and modernization. There was little middle ground.

The result of this historical experience is that the attitude of the ruling classes toward the Catholic Church is very different in Mexico from what it is in the United States. In the United States, the constitutional separation of church and state has to a great extent established boundaries that both sides find acceptable, and the dialogue is usually polite when differences develop. In Mexico, on the one hand, the long subordination of church to state has meant that the civil authorities expect the church to support them and are outraged when it challenges their judgment. On the other hand, the anti-clerical memories of the nineteenth century authorize the use of language that in the United States would be unacceptable in public discourse. The constant vilification of Don Samuel by the powerful of Chiapas is comprehensible only within this framework. They are scandalized at what they see as the bishop's desertion to the enemy.

In Mexico, as generally, the pendulum swung back and forth throughout the nineteenth century and into the twentieth. With Conservatives in power, the church acquired wealth and influence. It accumulated extensive properties, urban and rural, all tax-exempt and most unproductive. It functioned largely as a state within the state, with its own network of tribunals. It received the tithes that everyone was obligated to pay, when necessary invoking the state's help to collect them. It had a monopoly of education and maintained the country's only population records.

Resentment against such wealth and power finally brought the anti-clerical Liberals to power in the Revolution of 1910, and they undertook to eliminate the church as a social force. The project was implemented in the Constitution of 1917, which confiscated all church property, forbade the wearing of clerical dress in public, barred clerics from teaching, deprived them of the vote, and excluded them from election to public office. It also denied the church juridical personality and the right to hold property. Open persecution followed in the

1920s, especially after Plutarco Elías Calles became president in 1924. It seemed as if the coup de grâce had indeed been delivered.

Appearances, nevertheless, were deceptive. As the Revolution became more institutionalized and less revolutionary, a new informal *modus vivendi* was found. While the restrictive laws remained in force, they gradually ceased to be enforced. *Prestanombres* ("name lenders") enabled the church again to hold property, to operate schools at all levels from kindergarten through university, to build up major publishing operations, and to become once more an important component of public opinion.

❖

This situation might have continued indefinitely were it not for a change of policy in Rome during the pontificate of Pope John Paul II. Pope John XXIII and the Vatican Council had committed the church to a partnership of equals with all positive elements in human society in the task of building a more human world. John Paul II's Rome now sought to revert to an earlier age in which the church, in alliance with the state, would play a leadership role in civil society.

More specifically, Rome was looking for ways to deal with enormous geographic changes in church membership. How could it maintain control of a Latin American church containing half of all the world's Catholics?

The contours of the chosen solution have now become reasonably clear: reaffirm the principle of hierarchical authority, increasing ever more a centralized control over every aspect of church life; make blind obedience on sexual issues (seen as including clerical celibacy, remarriage of divorced, rejection of contraception and abortion) the criteria for selection of bishops and other church officials; promote Opus Dei, Communion and Liberation, the Legionaries of Christ, and other conservative movements, supported by such massive television operations as Lumen 2000, to control the masses. In a word, create a united, strong, centralized church, with dynamic apparatuses in local churches that would enable it to establish relations of power to power with governments. Essential to this vision is the elimination of all dissent within the church itself. Control must be monolithic. That meant that liberation theology, which had split the church in Latin America, had to be reformulated in ways that would be acceptable to governments with which Rome wanted to maintain or establish good relations.

With the arrival of Archbishop Girolamo Prigione as apostolic delegate in February 1978, Mexico became a major testing ground for this policy. Prigione's previous performance in the Holy See's diplomatic service identified him as pompous, cynical, arrogant, ambitious, at home with the wealthy. As nuncio to Guatemala and El Salvador at the height of the ethnocidal campaigns of Guatemala's military dictatorship, he had excellent relations with the generals. When the archdiocese of San Salvador fell vacant in 1977, he opposed the selection of the progressive Arturo Rivera y Damas, and secured the choice of the conservative Oscar Arnulfo Romero. Earlier, when assigned simultaneously to Nigeria and Ghana, he was very much at home with the rightist Nigerian government but so offended the leftist government of Ghana that he was declared *persona non grata*. He left West Africa amid rumors of involvement in illegal dealings in foreign exchange and black market ivory.

In Mexico, Prigione has worked astutely to build a solid bloc of bishops committed to the Vatican project and supportive of his personal ambitions. He set out methodically to isolate and marginalize the few bishops whose commitment to the indigenous brought them into conflict with state and federal governments. Three of these were in the state of Chihuahua, Adalberto Almeida (Chihuahua), Manuel Talamás Camandari (Ciudad Juárez), and José Llaguno Farías (vicariate of Tarahumara). Others in the same category, all in dioceses having a large indigenous population, were Arturo Lona Reyes (Tehuantepec), Bartolomé Carrasco (Oaxaca), and Samuel Ruiz. Finally there was Sergio Méndez Arceo

(Cuernavaca), who since the Vatican Council was the recognized leader of progressive Catholics in Mexico and a thorn in the side of successive presidents.

Prigione's first step in 1978 was to strip off part of the territory of Ciudad Juárez to create the prelature of Nuevo Casas Grandes, to which he named Hilario Chávez Joya, a traditionalist, as bishop. He next named Juan Sandoval Iñiguez as coadjutor to Ciudad Juárez, and Sandoval in due course succeeded on the enforced retirement of Manuel Talamás at age seventy-five. José Fernández Arteaga was similarly moved into Chihuahua, first as coadjutor then as successor to Adalberto Almeida, who retired in 1991. Death removed the doughty Méndez Arceo in 1992, and on the death of José Llaguno the following year, control of Tarahumara passed to Fernández Arteaga in nearby Chihuahua until a new bishop, José Luis Dibildox Martínez, was named there two years later.

By now, only Lona Reyes and Samuel Ruiz are left, and as we shall see, Prigione is determined to get rid of them too. He has a strong hand. In the fourteen years up to 1993 he chose fifty bishops and promoted twenty-five others. That means that at least seventy-five of Mexico's ninety bishops owe him a favor. He simultaneously established friendly relations with major politicians, including Patrocinio González Garrido, who as governor of Chiapas publicly identified Don Samuel as his greatest enemy.

❖

The Mexican government in the 1980s was engaged in a long-term strategy to create the political as well as the economic conditions that would ensure its admission to the U.S.-Canadian free trade area (NAFTA). A major obstacle was the pastoral activity of five or six bishops whose dioceses contained a substantial indigenous population. Largely through the efforts of Don Samuel as head of the Bishops Commission for the Indigenous, they had become a force at the national level on behalf of Mexico's indigenous, a group more numerous than those of any other country of Latin America. Since the government's project required, among other things, the ending of the *ejido* system, it was important to silence this voice.

Apostolic Delegate Prigione proved eminently willing to oblige in return for support for his own grand design, which was to establish official church-state relations, leading to a nunciature, all of which he finally obtained. In an unprece dented public denunciation of an apostolic delegate by a bishop, some of his tactics were put on the public record in 1991 by Bishop Arturo Lona Reyes of Tehuantepec, Oaxaca, in an interview given to *La Jornada*, a leading Mexico City daily. The apostolic delegate, Lona Reyes charged, had engaged in "a military strategy" to weaken, divide, and destroy the Pacific South pastoral program, a joint program of the dioceses with big indigenous populations. Because this program gave priority to accompanying the people and not to church-state relations, he said, "some of our colleagues but especially the apostolic delegate disapproved of it. We were never given pastoral support. Some of us were called Marxists, trouble-makers, undisciplined."[26]

Lona Reyes described at length the harassment he endured. He was humiliated, he said, by being subjected to an "apostolic visitation," a formal investigation by Vatican officials of his orthodoxy. They said the diocesan programs were "extremely horizontalized," making no mention of the transcendental, that the base communities were politicized, that Rome had not received reports on the state of the diocese since he became bishop in 1971. All of this, said the bishop, was "defamatory."

The issue of "horizontalization," which Don Samuel's enemies all raise in San Cristóbal, plays a major role in the criticisms of liberation theology issued by Cardinal Joseph Ratzinger's Congregation for the Doctrine of the Faith, successor to the Holy Office and the Sacred Inquisition, Rome's guardian of right thinking and protector of the faithful against heresy. For Ratzinger, one of the major dangers of the modern world is that it concentrates unduly on the quality of earthly life to the neglect of the vertical element, the relationship of the human with the transcendental God. On this issue Pope John Paul II sees eye to eye with Ratzinger. He thinks bishops like Lona Reyes and Ruiz have lost their sense of proportion. Of the late Bishop Leónidas Proaño of Riobamba, Ecuador, one of the first to emerge at and after the Vatican Council as a protector of the indigenous, he once said he was "obsessed with his Indians."[27]

The apostolic visitation, Lona Reyes said, was followed by an official letter from Cardinal Bernardin Gantin, head of the Vatican Congregation of Bishops, to come to Rome to answer the charges. "When I handed him copies of all the statistics and reports I had sent to Rome since 1971, he said 'What a shame you had to make this trip.' But afterward I was not exonerated from the charges and doubts. I am still a marked man."[28]

Lona Reyes interpreted his misfortunes as flowing logically from Vatican policy as crafted by Prigione. It would seem, he lamented, that the church of Mexico ended at Puebla (just south of Mexico City) and that the rest of the country, Oaxaca and Chiapas, has been abandoned. "These blows show that they do not approve of our accompaniment of the people. That is our crime."

On many occasions, Lona Reyes added, Prigione had pressured him to withdraw statements critical of the government, for example, his protests about the lack of sanitary facilities for migrant workers or the treatment of refugees from Guatemala. "He does not defend the bishop, but as a diplomat he supports the position of the government official. That makes me think that there is a give-and-take between them, a diplomatic negotiation." The link would become clearer when the time came, after the secondary figures had been marginalized, to open fire on the main trouble-maker, Samuel Ruiz.

Prigione has also publicly rebuked other bishops. The bishops of the state of Chihuahua and the bishop of Ciudad Juárez, for example, ordered *huelgas de culto* ("worship strikes," suspension of Sunday Masses), a form of interdict, to protest massive vote fraud in the 1986 presidential elections, in which Salinas de Cortari was proclaimed president. As Archbishop Adalberto Almeida of Chihuahua later revealed, Prigione intervened at the request of interior secretary and former governor of Chiapas Manuel Bartlett, persuading Cardinal Agostino Casaroli, Vatican secretary of state, to order the bishops to lift the interdict on the grounds that it violated canon law. The mayor of Chihuahua, Luis H. Álvarez, who had started a hunger strike because of the election fraud, was similarly approached by Prigione, who urged him to end his protest.

Nor was Prigione satisfied with having forced the bishops to call off the interdict. Within two years he taught them what it cost to challenge his authority. He had the Vatican impose on Archbishops Bartolomé Carrasco of Oaxaca and Adalberto Almeida of Chihuahua and on Bishop Manuel Talamás of Ciudad Juárez coadjutors with special faculties to control the clergy, limiting the bishops to handling business affairs.[29] Also a casualty was Bishop Rafael García of Tabasco, who had denounced PEMEX, the state petroleum monopoly, for environmental contamination and other abuses. He was transferred to the conservative diocese of León.

Another demonstration of the extent of Prigione's collaboration with the Mexican authorities in their efforts to keep "subversive" foreign priests and religious out of the country came to light in 1990. Cardinal Miguel Obando y Bravo was denied a visa to attend a meeting of the Conference of Mexican Bishops (CEM) in November of that year. After considerable investigation, it emerged that officials of the Interior Secretariat had established a practice of submitting to Prigione applications for visas made to Mexican consulates by religious personnel anywhere in Latin America, and on this occasion they could not reach him because he was out of the country. Subsequent investigations revealed that an Ecuadorian bishop, two priests, and a Brazilian nun had been denied visas to attend a conference on indigenous theology organized by the National Center of Aid to Indigenous Missions (CENAMI) and that immigration officials had told the conference organizers they needed to get a letter from Prigione for another sixty persons before they would be given visas.

In 1991 Prigione received his reward for his years of cooperation with the Mexican authorities. For the first time since the 1910 Revolution, the government established official relations with the Holy See. President Salinas named Agustín Téllez Cruces, retired head of the Supreme Court, as his personal representative to Pope John Paul II, and he received Archbishop Prigione as the pope's personal representative to the president. It was less than diplomatic recognition, but that would come in September 1992, when Mexico and the Holy See established formal diplomatic relations and Prigione presented his credentials as nuncio.

❖

Also in 1991, the conflict between Don Samuel and Chiapan governor Patrocinio González Garrido made national and international headlines. A member of one of the wealthiest and most powerful families of ranchers in Chiapas, González was a formidable adversary. Antonio Ortiz Mena, his father-in-law and uncle of President Salinas, who had been head of the Inter-American Development Bank for seventeen years, was chosen in 1988 by Salinas to head BANAMEX, one of Mexico's biggest banks, which had been nationalized in 1982. These connections at the level of the federal government would soon vault González to the key post of interior secretary, in charge of internal security.

Angered by the bishop's charges, made at the prestigious Center for Theological Reflection in Mexico City, of a "disturbing growth of repression" in Chiapas, González arrested Joel Padrón González, one of Don Samuel's priests. Padrón, the governor charged, had committed half a dozen crimes, including robbery, looting, carrying illegal arms, organizing gangs, and inciting his parishioners to occupy land illegally. A group of cattle ranchers told the judge, when Padrón was arraigned, that the pulpits were being used to promote violence. The local newspaper, *Diario de Chiapas*, not only gave editorial approval for the arrest but listed by name five other priests as next in line for judicial action. This initiative of the governor, it said, should help to clarify the role of the priest and should get Eriberto Cruz Vera in Las Margaritas, Gustavo Andrade in Palenque, Antonio de Tenejapa in Amatán, Tacho de Belisario Domínguez in Motozintla, and Eduardo Ruiz in Larraínzar to mend their ways. Given the level of corruption in the courts, there is no effective recourse for one who is libeled by the powerful in Chiapas.

The warning that he might lose another half dozen priests did not shake Don Samuel. He rejected out of hand an offer from González to release Father Joel in return for a retraction of the bishop's denunciation of violations of human rights in Chiapas. Instead, he named Padrón to the post of diocesan director of prison ministry and set out to give the incident national and international publicity. Neither the Bishops Conference nor the apostolic delegate supported him, but in the end Don Samuel prevailed. After three months the charges were dropped and Father Joel returned to a triumphant welcome in his parish.

Meanwhile, Prigione was actively cultivating the contacts with the top leadership of the governing party, the PRI, which he needed for the constitutional changes that would permit establishment of full diplomatic relations. It was not always smooth going. Some statements made by Pope John Paul II during his 1990 visit to Mexico, for example, suggested a lack of enthusiasm on the part of Rome for the government policies that were widening the gap between rich and poor. At Durango, he commented that it was often the poor who were forced to make sacrifices, while those with great fortunes were reluctant to renounce their privileges for the common good. The theme was taken up by several leading churchmen. Bishop Genaro Alamilla, retired bishop of Papantla and former head of the Bishops Conference, deplored at a meeting of businessmen the growing accumulation of wealth by big business and government.

In spite of such setbacks, Prigione held to his course, and in 1991 he achieved a major breakthrough by winning the cooperation of the Mexican bishops for the key element in the government's modernization program, the North American Free Trade Agreement (NAFTA). Seven Mexican bishops joined six of their U.S. colleagues in May of that year in Washington for a briefing by U.S. trade representative Carla Hills during a "summit" meeting on NAFTA of U.S. and Mexican government, business, and church leaders.

The government had understandably to pay a price for the bishops' support of NAFTA. In his third State of the Union address in November 1991, President Salinas began to prepare the public for the reward he would give the bishops, namely, legal recognition of the church. But to deliver on that promise, which required a constitutional amendment, he needed to win a two-thirds majority of deputies in the 1992 elections, and that required a higher than usual manipulation of votes. The rigging of these elections was so blatant that even the Social Affairs Commission (CEPS) of the bishops supported the charges of fraud brought by the opposition parties. In the end, however, the protests were swept under the table as usual, and the PRI got its two-thirds majority.

❖

The dream of Prigione and the overwhelming majority of the bishops was finally realized in January 1992 when five articles of the Constitution were amended. Most of the anti-church provisions in the 1917 Constitution were eliminated. Separation of church and state was reaffirmed, the state defined as neither religious nor anti-religious, churches as dedicated to their mission and playing no role in party politics. Churches and religious associations were granted juridic status and were enabled to acquire legal personality through a system of registration. Private schools were authorized to teach religion. The right of religious orders to exist was recognized. Religious entities could hold the property needed to fulfil their functions. Ministers of religion were allowed to vote, but not to run for office. All Catholics approved of the changes as being in themselves desirable and just. Many, nevertheless, had two reservations. They felt the people should have been consulted. They also felt that the concessions had been bought at too great a price.

The Conference of Religious, the official organization of the religious priests, brothers, and sisters who constitute the vast majority of the Mexican church's professionals, led the criticism. In an evaluation that was leaked to the press, the governing board charged that, in return for constitutional changes that are "token and irrelevant," the bishops have pulled back from defending the human rights of the poor.

The church, they argued, had agreed to "reprivatize" itself, in the same way as the Mexican regime was reprivatizing not only industry but also education (the cost of which it was no longer prepared to pay), reprivatization being the current technique for increasing the wealth of those already rich. For the church it meant getting back into the sacristy, concentrating on service to the business élites, abandoning industrial and agricultural workers, and developing schools for the children of the wealthy, with the risk of giving up its evangelizing mission to the poor in public education. "A hierarchy forced to reprivatize its activities and limit them to the élites of the neocapitalist culture" offers even less social challenge than did a church that, "although juridically unrecognized, enjoyed in fact a privileged and unusual freedom."[30]

Retired bishop of Cuernavaca Méndez Arceo was even more outspoken in his criticism of the church-state agreement. "I don't know if the church was better off under Diocletian [who persecuted it] or under Constantine [who recognized it]," he commented. Méndez Arceo and Prigione had long been enemies. Prigione's famous comment about him was that "he sings outside the choir."[31]

The bishops angrily repudiated the charges brought by the Conference of Religious. Its position, they said, constituted "a classical parallel magisterium." The expression "parallel magisterium" is a favorite of Cardinal Ratzinger when he condemns any theological opinion that questions the official Roman line. The bishops were saying in effect that it was their privilege to make decisions without consulting the rest of the church.

Other constitutional reforms voted at the same time, especially the amendment of Article 27, brought anguished screams from all those concerned with the lot of the poor. Don Samuel, supported by Archbishop Bartolomé Carrasco of Oaxaca and Bishop Arturo Lona of Tehuantepec, Oaxaca, led the protests. At a conference in San Cristóbal he deplored the Article 27 provision allowing the sale of *ejido* lands and their use as collateral by individual members. This was, he said, an effort by the government to reconcentrate land in the hands of a few for the benefit of monopoly agribusiness. The provision that no further petitions for registration of *ejido* titles would be accepted was seen as particularly harmful for the indigenous of Chiapas. Very many of the *ejidos* in the state had filed for title and received preliminary approval, but the bureaucracy had never issued the documents.

That the state, in turn, would demand its pay-off for the benefits it had accorded the institutional church was soon apparent. Having achieved in 1992 his ambition of establishing full diplomatic relations and of being named nuncio, Prigione turned his big guns on Don Samuel who — during the pope's 1993 visit to Mexico — made a more public condemnation of that country's human rights record than ever before. The timing of Don Samuel's attack particularly outraged the Mexican authorities. They had been actively engaged in polishing Mexico's international image in anticipation of the critical vote in the U.S. Congress on NAFTA, and they had planned the papal visit precisely to promote the image of a modern, democratic, and civilized state. As this was the first time that the pope had come to Mexico to be received with all the honors of a head of state, the publicity surrounding Don Samuel's intervention was all the greater. He was playing for high stakes.

# Chapter 5

# MEXICO SEEN FROM BELOW

I T CERTAINLY was not very politic. But, then, Don Samuel was never very politic. Here was an elaborate conspiracy, in which civil and religious leaders of Mexico were accomplices, the purpose of which was to give the pope and all world opinion an utterly distorted picture of the reality in which the poor of Mexico were living. How could he be silent? Someone had to shout out loud that the emperor was naked.

This was, in a sense, the moment for which Don Samuel had long been waiting, the opportunity to tell, not just the pope, but the people of Mexico and indeed the people of the world what he had learned as bishop of San Cristóbal de Las Casas. As usual, he engaged in extensive consultation before acting. The groundwork had been laid in an assembly of the Pueblo Creyente ("believing people"), a diocesan advisory group, in May. There, agreement was reached as to what were the significant events in the diocese during the thirty-four years of Don Samuel's pastorate.

The meeting took place at Izamal, near Mérida on the Yucatán peninsula, in the presence of some six thousand representatives of the indigenous of the American continent. Izamal, once an important religious center of the Maya civilization, had been chosen for the first major address of the papal visit. But the pope's somewhat conventional message to the indigenous took second place to the message of the in-

71

digenous — delivered by the bishop of San Cristóbal — to the pope. Entitled "In This Hour of Grace," the pastoral letter described for the visitor the country he was visiting, as that country's actions reflected on the lives of the people of the diocese of San Cristóbal de Las Casas.[32] Here we have the distillation of the years of reflection of Don Samuel and his co-workers on their reality. The voiceless have at last a voice that is heard around the globe.

In Chiapas, Don Samuel told the pope, the indigenous live in a state of dependency. They are oppressed and pushed to the margins of national life, not because they are inferior or inadequate, but because such is the deliberate choice and positive decision of the small group of power brokers who control all branches of government, legislative, judicial, and executive. It was a situation the bishop could talk about with solid credentials. He had devoted his ministry to creating an awareness among his people and accompanying them in their efforts to organize, only to run up at every point against a government that was committed to defend the strong against the weak.

The first section analyzes the material and social condition of the diocese. Identifying himself completely with his people, the bishop says that "we" are facing ever greater oppression and hardship, "living in cheerless silence and at times in despair, . . . trapped in a way of life and of work that oppresses us." Privatizations and the Free Trade Agreement (NAFTA) are needed to enable the strongest and most powerful groups, both national and foreign, to increase their wealth while abandoning campesinos and laborers to their fate.

"We are a dependent country at the level of the state, the municipality, the *ejido,* and the village. This dependency can be broken only by starting at the periphery, when the marginalized and oppressed form themselves into a conscious and organized people. The state does not permit this to happen, because it would smash its hegemonic project; in consequence, it seeks to prevent the people from achieving self-awareness or organization, and to keep them in subjection by means of political, economic, ideological, and politico-military controls."

Instead of responding to the need for land and work, the government attempts to maintain order without justice, changing laws and inventing new crimes, creating a system that is by its nature a violator of human rights. Shortages, unemployment, injustice, and misery grow. Structures are created to squeeze the poor. Voting is manipulated. If a popular candidate wins, the election is nullified. In the countryside we have no electricity, potable water, or sewers. If health services are provided, they are mostly for birth control and abortion. Alcoholism, a sign of frustration, is widespread. Discrimination and inequality are rife in the administration of justice and in disrespect for human rights. Court processes and electoral procedures, controlled by the government and its party, lack credibility. For years the church in San Cristóbal has collected data on the fabrication of offenses, illegal arrests, tortures, impunity for wrongdoers, unjust imprisonments, ill treatment in jails, evictions. In Chiapan society, inequality affects all human and social relations, burdening them with a load of oppression and domination that constitutes part of the collective consciousness.

The poverty comes from structures created over five hundred years. Land reform had its moment in Chiapas when Lázaro Cárdenas was president (1934–40), but after him it slowed down, and peonage continued into the 1980s. The debt crisis then resulted in the neoliberal adjustment processes, the negative impact of which was greatest on the poorest. The indigenous do not have the land they need to grow their food. Requests for land go unanswered, and land that is offered is too expensive to buy. Some own much land that they leave idle. The oil wells also take much land out of production. Chiapas is now the victim of the second modernization of the Chiapan countryside, with the reform of Article 27 of the Constitution (privatization of the *ejido*) converting land into a merchandise and facilitating its purchase by highly capitalized businesses. The result is "a breaking down of the community sense of land, its concentration into ever larger holdings, and migration to the cities." The indigenous, despoiled of their land, "become strangers in their own home."

Prices for what the indigenous produce are low. Middlemen are avaricious and thieves. Wages are so low that they do not meet minimum family needs. Wage disputes are always resolved in favor of the employer. Taxes are high. The indigenous are humiliated and tricked. They are forced to vote for the government party, the PRI. They are not allowed to organize, and the authorities choose and impose the local officials who are supposed to be elected. Corruption reigns at all levels, and the police and army oppress the people in the towns and in the countryside. Illiteracy is widespread. Teachers are irresponsible, education is deficient, and school supplies are expensive. There is neither electricity, drinking water, nor drainage.

Given this context, it is not surprising that the diocese has known much conflict in recent decades. Having analyzed their reality, the indigenous have been building their own organizations and developing techniques for struggle that will help them obtain land and better living conditions, and the beneficiaries of the status quo have been responding with violence. "In the society of Chiapas, inequality is integral to all human and social relations, impregnating them with a burden of oppression and domination that forms part of the collective conscience."

❖

Don Samuel next turned to the subject that the Mexican government least wanted to be highlighted during the papal visit. Recent weeks, he wrote, have seen our country involved in a series of very alarming happenings that show how narcotraffic has entered the police, the judicial, and the political structures. Many say that while this situation persists, democratization will remain a dream, with the risk of extra-institutional clashes.

There were several reasons why the drug issue, and especially the suggestion of related "extra-institutional clashes," Colombia-style, was embarrassing. As part of its propaganda for the upcoming vote on the North American Free Trade Agreement (NAFTA) in the U.S. Congress, the Mexican government was trying to show that it was clamping down on the drugs moving north through Mexico from Peru, Bolivia, and Colombia, and in particular on the domestic production of poppies that had in recent years made Mexico a major producer of opium for sale in the United States.

Even more challenging was Don Samuel's reference to the assassination of Cardinal Juan Jesús Posadas Ocampo. The circumstances of the killing suggested that the cardinal, who for some time had been very outspoken in his condemnation of the drug trade, might have been the chosen victim of a drug cartel. This was the last thing that either the Mexican government or the papal nuncio wanted the pope to hear. They were agreed, for their different reasons, to persuade the pope that the assassination of Posadas three months earlier had not been intentional but simply a case of mistaken identity. The official government story, although endorsed by Prigione, was widely questioned. Many members of the Catholic hierarchy, as well as others, suspected that people high in government were involved.

This was not the first time that Don Samuel had charged the government with complicity in the drug trade. A pastoral letter in March 1984, which he co-signed with the other bishops of the Southern Pacific region, denounced the violations of the human rights of the campesinos by the army and federal narcotics agents. They charged "top government officials" with complicity in drug trafficking and with ignoring drug lords who were the biggest offenders. Similar charges were made at various times by bishops or church-related entities. In June 1993, for example, shortly before the visit of Pope John Paul, a newsletter of the archdiocese of Oaxaca reported that "the drug traffic has bought or entered partnership with a significant number of public functionaries and military personnel."

The still mystery-clouded death of Posadas was also something that Nuncio Prigione — as later emerged — would have preferred to have seen drop into oblivion. But Don Samuel was determined to raise the issue as evidence of the corruption in high places that hurt the poor of his diocese. Among other things, it was they who, when they cultivated poppies or marijuana in the absence of other ways to make a living, were jailed and beaten, while corrupt law officers let the traffickers go free.

❖

Following his devastating challenge to the official depiction given the pope of the state of the nation, the bishop proceeded to describe where the diocese of San Cristóbal stands, and why. The public attacks on the bishop and his fellow workers by Prigione, González Garrido, and the *Familia Chiapaneca* had made this necessary.

A long process of conversion after the Second Vatican Council had committed the diocese to place itself on the margins of society in the company of its poor members, he wrote. By doing this, it was faithful to its sixteenth-century bishop, Fray Bartolomé de Las Casas, defender of the indigenous. The process was a complicated one. The diocese had to develop an indigenous pastoral approach, understood not merely as requiring a preoccupation with the indigenous, but as a true incarnation of its presence in their world. That world lacks many things, but it also has great values. Being part of it directs the diocese's reflection on faith, its pastoral activity, and our ecclesial hope toward the creation of an autochthonous or indigenous church. The church envisaged will express itself in the culture of the people, will enrich itself with their values, embrace their sufferings, struggles, and aspirations, will transform and liberate their culture with the power of the gospel.

The rationale for this vision, the bishop continued, was expressed by an indigenous man to an apostolic delegate many years ago. "If the church," he said, "does not make itself Tzeltal with the Tzeltales, Chol with the Choles, Tojolabal with the Tojolabales, I don't see how it can call itself catholic." It would be an alien church, belonging to the dominant social class, a stranger to the indigenous. The religious schizophrenia the indigenous have lived since the war of conquest will not disappear until they enjoy this kind of inculturation of the gospel, giving its fruits at the hands of their own ministers, in the reflection of their faith through their own cultural media, in celebration of the sacraments presented with external signs that have meaning within their own cultural traditions.

The bishop next analyzed the connection between the pastoral commitment of the diocese to the indigenous and the harassment of which he has been the target at the hands both of the state and of the economically and socio-culturally privileged sectors. Calumny and lies have been spread, he wrote, by the official and para-official media. Pastoral agents have been imprisoned. Catechists have been killed. Accusations have even come from church sources, involving manipulation and deception.

The letter ends with a brief account of the results of the pastoral program of the diocese. The indigenous and campesino communities have come a long way toward becoming subjects of their own history, no longer the objects of decisions made by others. They have acquired a consciousness of dignity fed by evangelical values. They are occupying the space that is theirs by right in the church, and therefore in history. They have increased their esteem for their own languages, their legitimate customs, and their cultural identity. Under the supervision of the diocese, which has final responsibility, Scripture translations into the various languages have been made by translators chosen by the communities. They have organized many kinds of cooperatives, health facilities, and training courses.

The bishop acknowledges many errors in the pastoral pilgrimage of the diocese. Its first actions, before the Second Vatican Council, were destructive of culture, he wrote. It had only its own — ethnocentric and moralistic — criteria to judge customs. In consequence, without realizing it, it was on the side of the oppressors.

The mission of the diocese, nevertheless, was not only to the poor. In an obvious response to the criticisms expressed by Prigione and others that he was biased against the *criollos*, he notes, with sadness, his many unsuccessful attempts to open the eyes of the oppressors. "We have not found a way — if there is one — to reach those who are geographically close to the indigenous but far from them in their hearts."

The closing paragraph of the letter merits quotation: "Our objective is to ensure that our diocesan church proclaim, in union with the universal and the Latin American church, the practice of Jesus and life in a participative and fraternal community, committing itself to the people and serving them, inserting itself like Jesus in the process of liberation of the oppressed, a church in which they will be makers of their own history so that together we may build the new society as a precursor of the Kingdom."

❖

Though met with stunned official silence, Don Samuel's broadside understandably received major attention in the national newspapers. It was an open declaration of war on the policies of the federal government toward Chiapas. "Such a report in the pope's hands," one commentator noted, "runs counter to the policy of the government and that of the nuncio."[33]

Don Samuel's reference to the assassination of Cardinal Juan Jesús Posadas Ocampo was widely commented on. Posadas, who was a confidant of the nuncio and was also close to President Salinas, had been a major apologist for the conservative wing of the Mexican hierarchy. The progressive priests in his diocese criticized his luxurious lifestyle.

When he had replaced Sergio Méndez Arceo as bishop of Cuernavaca, he refused to ordain the clerics who had been trained in the spirit of Méndez Arceo at the Higher Institute of Church Studies, and they had to find other bishops to accept them. If Ruiz wanted the circumstances of his death clarified, it was not because of any personal sympathy with the cardinal.

Posadas had been killed in a blast of automatic weapons fire as he approached Guadalajara airport in a white Grand Marquis in May 1993. His driver and five other individuals died with him. He was coming to welcome Nuncio Prigione, who was about to arrive from Mexico City.

The assassination understandably made national headlines. Guadalajara is the second most important diocese in the country after Mexico City, and its apostolic resources are greater than those of any other Latin American diocese: a thousand priests, three seminaries, and six million (at least nominal) faithful.

Why Posadas was killed has never been established, but the rumor mills immediately hinted a relation with the drug cartels. Mexico's attorney general Jorge Carpizo agreed that drugs were involved, but not in the way the rumors suggested. The cardinal, he said, was caught in crossfire between rival drug gangs.

An ingenious suggestion, people said, but not convincing. While it is now generally agreed that gunmen in the service of drug lords killed the cardinal, what remains in dispute is whether his death was intended or resulted from mistaken identity. That there was never crossfire between hostile gangs, as the attorney general claimed, seems clear. The only gunmen present were employees of Ramón and Benjamín Arellano Félix, brothers who controlled a major drug cartel in Tijuana, where Posadas had previously been bishop. Nobody attempted to arrest the eight gunmen as they sauntered from the scene and nonchalantly entered the airport. Although they had no boarding passes, they were allowed to leave on a scheduled Aeroméxico flight to Tijuana, a flight that was delayed for more than twenty minutes to enable them to catch it.

Attorney General Carpizo's official report, however, presents a radically different scenario. Gunmen, he said, mistook the cardinal's white Grand Marquis luxury sedan (a model popular with drug lords), for the car of rival drug trafficker Joaquín "El Chapo" Guzmán Loera, who in fact arrived almost simultaneously at the airport. Guzmán, Carpizo said, had a carefully prepared plan to eliminate the entire Arellano Félix gang.[34]

Unconvinced by the attorney general's explanation, Archbishop Héctor González of Oaxaca and four other members of the social affairs commission of the Mexican bishops issued a pastoral letter in June charging that narcotics trafficking mafia had bought off or associated with a considerable number of public and military officials. Protests from the Defense Ministry, which saw the allegation as an attempt to involve the army in the Posadas scandal, succeeded in getting the bishops to withdraw the charge.

New questions were soon raised, however, by Archbishop (now Cardinal) Juan Sandoval Iñiguez, shortly after he was installed as archbishop of Guadalajara in May 1994. A half-dozen eyewitnesses to the cardinal's killing, he said, were willing to testify if their identities were concealed. Some of them were Jehovah's Witnesses who went each day to the airport to hand out leaflets and promote their beliefs. Their eyewitness evidence, as reported, was that two hours before the cardinal was killed, they had seen an unusually large force of police arrive. They had no idea at that point why the extra police had come, but they later associated their presence with the expected arrival of the nuncio. When Cardinal Posadas pulled up at the airport terminal, they said, the gunmen went straight to his vehicle and fired directly at him. The evidence of "an unusually large force of police" at the airport, who could hardly not have heard the shooting, adds to the mystery of the gunmen's leisurely escape.

The law enforcement authorities had asked Archbishop

Sandoval to share with them any relevant information he might find. To his surprise, when he delivered the testimonies he had collected to the attorney general's office, he was told to stop interfering. Assistant Attorney General Mario Ruiz Massieu held a press conference to say the testimony was useless, and he told the archbishop to stop making unfounded and frivolous statements. In the climate of suspicion and conflicting interpretations, such an answer from one closely related to President Salinas was understandably read as expressing an official intention to leave the mystery unsolved.

Others who rejected the official explanation included Genaro Alamilla, retired bishop of Papantla and ex-spokesman for the Mexican bishops, Archbishop Carlos Quintero Arce of Hermosillo, Archbishop Abelardo Alvarado Alcántara, auxiliary of Mexico City, Bishop Norberto Rivera Carrera of Tehuacán, Bishop Rafael García González of León, and Archbishop (now Cardinal) Juan Sandoval Iñiguez.

Various Catholic organizations similarly challenged the official explanation. They included the National Union of Fathers of Families, the Testimony and Hope Movement, the National Pro-Life Committee, the Christian Family Movement, and Communion and Liberation. They pointed out that nobody could have mistaken the cardinal for "El Chapo" Guzmán because of the difference in age and physique. The killers had a clear view of him. The forensic expert had testified that fourteen bullets had been fired from so close up that there were powder burns on the cardinal's clothing.

Nuncio Prigione, nevertheless, continued to defend the government position, and he also had his supporters in the hierarchy. When Pope John Paul II visited Mexico in August 1993, the Permanent Commission of the Mexican Bishops Conference (President Adolfo Suárez Rivera, Secretary General Godínez Flores, Bishop Gilberto Valbuena Sánchez of Colima, and Bishop José Esaúl Robles of Zamora) joined him in handing a report accepting the official version to the pope.

"We recognize and appreciate the efforts made by our authorities to prosecute, not only as their duty but also out of their personal conviction, this and similar crimes."[35]

In this context, Don Samuel's decision to bring charges of official involvement in the drug trade and his linking of narcotraffic to the assassination of Posadas in the letter he handed to visiting Pope John Paul II, was upping the ante in his challenge to the government and — as later emerged — to Prigione.

It was not until July 1994, nearly a year later, that the nuncio was linked publicly to the Posadas mystery by three articles written by Rafael Medina in the Mexico City daily *Excelsior*. Citing documentation given him by Benjamín Arellano Félix, one of the two brothers identified as heads of the Tijuana drug cartel, Medina charged that the nuncio was part of a network of co-conspirators that reached all the way to the president of Mexico. Prigione, he said, had been in communication with the Tijuana cartel in June 1993, the month after the cardinal's assassination. Ramón Arellano went to talk to the nuncio in the nunciature on December 1, 1993, and Benjamín's visit was on the 16th of the following month. At that time the brothers had already been publicly identified as the employers of the gunmen who had killed Posadas, and they were on three "Most Wanted" lists: in Mexico, in the United States, and at INTERPOL. During the meeting with Ramón, Prigione left him at his residence while he went to discuss what he had learned with President Salinas, Interior Secretary Patrocinio González Garrido, and Attorney General Jorge Carpizo.

The meetings with the nuncio, according to the *Excelsior* account, had been arranged by Gerardo Montaño Rubio, a priest of the diocese of Tijuana. Montaño, who was present at both interviews, was said to have been friendly with the Arellano brothers since the time he was fundraising for a new seminary for Posadas, then bishop of Tijuana. Before the meetings at the nunciature, he told *Excelsior*, he had given Prigione "closed and sealed" envelopes addressed to Pope

John Paul II, the contents of which have not been divulged. At the meetings, the Arellanos provided alibis to show they were in Tijuana at the time of the killing. The relevance of the alibis is unclear, since it had never been alleged that they themselves had been the killers.

Nuncio Prigione has changed his account of these meetings several times. His first response to reporters indicated that he didn't even know the Arellano brothers, that they had come to confess their sins and had made a sacramental confession. "Pardon is a very delicate conscience matter," he is quoted as having said. "Many people come to confess to me, and there is no reason why I should know all of them, . . . nor do I even ask them who they are."[36]

Later he admitted that he had known them. Their meetings, he said, dealt with personal matters. He had not given them sacramental absolution and consequently was not under the *sigillum* (canonical obligation of absolute silence); but, nevertheless, his sense of professional secrecy prevented him from disclosing the content of their discussions. He would restrict himself to saying that they had admitted no guilt and that he had advised them to turn themselves in to the authorities.

Prigione decided to change his story once again in early 1995 after Cardinal Sandoval Iñiguez, who had just had a conversation with Pablo Chapa Benzanilla, a special attorney then in charge of the investigation, told the press that it is becoming daily clearer that the murder was intentional. The nuncio said that he is now willing to talk to the special investigator, if he is subpoenaed.

Not surprisingly, the *Excelsior* revelations produced a crop of rumors. When a reporter asked Adolfo Suárez Rivera, president of the Bishops Conference, if he would comment on the claim that the nuncio was involved in alms laundering of narco money, he told him to go and find out for himself.[37]

Even some prominent Catholics, led by Antonio Roqueñí Ornelas, who had power of attorney to sign official documents for Cardinal Corripio of Mexico City, publicly criticized the nuncio's secret meeting with two men identified by the attorney general's office as the top suspects in the cardinal's assassination. Roqueñí had already in mid-January 1994 gone to the nunciature located on His Holiness John Paul II Street, to the south of Mexico City. He was accompanied by Enrique González Torres, director of the Foundation for Community Support. As they later told the press, they had consulted with the fifteen hundred priests of the archdiocese of Mexico City and representatives of the more than a thousand parishes and churches of the city, as well as several bishops who had approved of their plan but were unwilling to be identified.

At the interview, they urged Prigione to resign, telling him he had caused much confusion by not distinguishing between his role as ambassador of the Holy See and that of papal representative to the Mexican bishops. He was blocking the investigation into the assassination of Cardinal Posadas and interfering in internal politics of Mexico. He was an obstacle to the restoration of peace in Chiapas, they also told him, because of his hard line with Mexican bishops, especially Samuel Ruiz, and because he was maneuvering to have himself rather than Don Samuel named as intermediary in the proposed negotiations with the Zapatistas. In his efforts to discredit Don Samuel he had gone so far as to tell the *New York Times* and other publications that the church of Chiapas was to blame for the Zapatista uprising.[38]

Roqueñí raised one other issue during the interview that is important for understanding Prigione's campaign against Don Samuel, namely, Prigione's opposition to any church involvement in favor of Mexico's indigenous peoples. In early December 1993, Prigione had announced that the vicariate of Tarahumara, which had been in charge of Jesuit missionaries for more than three centuries, was being made into a diocese, that the diocesan seat was being moved from Sisoguichi to Guachochi, and that the bishop would be José Luis Dibildox Martínez, a diocesan priest of San Luis Potosí who had always worked in urban parishes and had absolutely no contact with the indigenous peoples. Dibildox, fifty years old, of Basque-French ancestry, did his graduate studies in the Catholic Institute of Paris. All bishops of the vicariate had been Jesuits.

The bishops of the six dioceses of the Northern Pastoral Region, who according to normal church protocol would have been consulted, all made it known that they were unhappy with the choice of Dibildox. Retired archbishop of Chihuahua Adalberto Almeida Merino told the press that Dibildox lacked the experience needed for this very special mission. The bishop of Tarahumara has to speak the language, said Juan Sandoval Iñiguez (then bishop of Ciudad Juárez), because the Tarahumaras constitute more than half the population of the diocese.

Jesuit provincial Jesús Morales Orozco was another who publicly protested the decision to change the status of the vicariate "in spite of the contrary view of all the pastoral agents" and to move the episcopal seat from Sisoguichi, an indigenous town, to Guachochi, a mestizo town. This, he said, has been interpreted as a way to reverse the pastoral program promoted by the former bishop (who had died two years before) with the support of all the priests and religious of the vicariate, a program incultured and committed to the defense of the human rights of the Tarahumaras.

On learning through the *Excelsior* revelations that Prigione had talked in the nunciature to Benjamín Arellano Félix the very day after he had urged him to resign, Roqueñí Ornelas exploded. "Had he no choice but to receive the suspected criminals who were being sought by all the police of the world? ... It is his duty to collaborate with the authorities and not get involved with a strictly national problem."[39]

The damage to the credibility of the Mexican government was enormous. At the very moment when the security forces were supposed to be engaged in a massive search for the drug lords as suspects in the Posadas murder, the president and the interior secretary were negotiating about them with the papal nuncio, and none of the three had felt an obligation to report what they were doing. Certainly their cloak-and-dagger style was very different from that of Don Samuel, who consistently submits his judgment to the challenge of public evaluation and discussion.

# Chapter 6

# PRIGIONE TELLS RUIZ TO RESIGN

N O ATTEMPT was made during or immediately after the papal visit to rebut the charges contained in Don Samuel's letter. Comment would only increase the damaging coverage by the media. But those familiar with the Byzantine ways of Mexican diplomacy did not doubt that the insult would not pass ignored. And it was not long before they were proved right. As Don Samuel himself commented in his Christmas 1993 pastoral letter, the letter to the pope was "apparently the drop of water that brought down the accumulated hatred of the power structures that live by exploiting the humble." But if the pastoral letter was not enough, it was followed up in September by a visit of Father Pablo Romo Cedano, head of the diocesan human rights center, to Washington, D.C., where he testified on abuses of human rights in Chiapas before the Small Business Committee of the House of Representatives and met with NAFTA opponent Congressman David Bonior and other businessmen.

The first hint of Nuncio Prigione's intentions came shortly after the end of the papal visit, when Prigione visited the head of the military detachment in San Cristóbal without either notifying the bishop or calling on him. He did this at a moment when the bishop was the object of an avalanche of threats and pressures from powerful groups in the state of Chiapas, local authorities, land speculators, ranchers, timber operators, and hotel and restaurant groups, all angry because of the pastoral letter.

Prigione's breach of protocol could hardly have been inadvertent. He is too experienced a diplomat. Another snub followed in October while Don Samuel was participating in a course for bishops in São Paulo, Brazil. As Miguel Angel Granados Chapa reported in a Mexico City newspaper, the nuncio had made an amazing statement two evenings earlier.[40] At a reception at the nunciature to commemorate the anniversary of the election of John Paul II to the papacy in 1976, he stated in after-dinner conversation that Samuel Ruiz García would shortly be removed from San Cristóbal.

Granados went on to describe at some length the commitment of the diocese to the poor and the conflicts with the local oligarchs and with state and national governments resulting from its support and defense of the indigenous. "This is a political event," he concluded, "that incarnates the struggle between the two churches, that which is associated with political power, and that which wishes to retain its independence and remain at the side of the poor."

Many were shocked at what they regarded a breach, not only of protocol, but of ethics, in the casual release of such damaging information without first notifying the church leader affected.

In the midst of rumors that the bishop had been told to resign or had been removed, a representative group from San Cristóbal, called together by diocesan officials to analyze the situation, sent a delegation to the nuncio. "The diocese of San Cristóbal is very conflictive," Prigione told the delegation, "not just now, but it has been for twenty years, and the Vatican is very concerned with the bishop's errors." These grave errors, were "doctrinal, pastoral, and administrative. They clash with the ministry of the church and offend the pope." At a press conference on October 20, Prigione repeated the same charges, adding that the issue is not what the bishop said in the diocese but what he said abroad. He did not explain further what prompted this comment. The "errors,"

Prigione had just said, were all related to his work in his diocese. Why then should the issue be "what he said abroad"? Is it possible that Prigione unintentionally revealed what really underlay the effort to get rid of Don Samuel: not his "doctrinal, pastoral, and administrative errors," but the fact that he now commanded national attention when he denounced the government's violations of human rights?

In Mexico City, on his way home from Brazil, the bishop on October 26 visited the nuncio, to be told that the Vatican had asked that he voluntarily submit his resignation. Without showing the text to Don Samuel, the nuncio read from a letter, which he said he had received from Cardinal Bernardin Gantin, head of the curial Congregation for Bishops. The letter was dated September 23, a time when the nuncio was visiting Rome. The bishop said later that the nuncio had told him that the cardinal had accused him of being guilty of very serious errors, doctrinal, pastoral, and administrative, errors that are in conflict with the church and affront the Holy Father.

❖

As the news spread, expressions of support for Don Samuel immediately began to pour in, not only from Mexico but from all parts of the world. Within twenty-four hours FAXes arrived from as far away as France, Korea, and Australia. Among the hundreds of organizations that expressed their indignation were the Conference of Religious Institutes, the Latin American Peace and Justice Service (SERPAJ), the Latin American Collective of Special Communication Services (CLASEC), the National Center of Social Communication (CENCOS), the Mexican Academy of Human Rights, the Ecumenical Center for Orientation and Formation, the Antonio Montesinos Center (Nicaragua), the Regional Center of Ecumenical Information (CRIE), Women Fighting for Democracy, Women for Dialogue, the Support Center for Working Women, the Mexican UN Association, the Mexican Committee for Defense and Advancement of Human

Rights, the Ecological Groups Pact, and the Mexican Program for Aid to Latin American Refugees. Angry telephone calls and FAXes poured into the nunciature in such a volume that Prigione changed his telephone and FAX numbers.

Individuals who publicly defended Don Samuel included the bishops of Tuxtla, Tapachula, Tehuantepec, and Texcoco, two retired archbishops, two retired bishops, the superiors of the Jesuits and of the Dominicans, Rigoberta Menchú, and Miguel Concha. "We support you fully" was the message in a letter signed by 102 superiors general and provincials of congregations of women and 25 provincials of congregations of men.

Rigoberta Menchú, who a short time before had invited Don Samuel to join her at the ceremony in Switzerland at which she received the Nobel Peace Prize, told the pope that if they silence "this distinguished voice of indigenous peoples," Rome would be repeating the error it had made in the case of Bartolomé de Las Casas in the sixteenth century. "With words and deeds they [the bishop and diocese] have opened their heart and home to my brothers and sisters in exile. With words and deeds they have proclaimed the gospel of Jesus to our indigenous brothers and sisters of Mexico and to those in exile struggling to survive the repression.... Personally, I will be in debt all my life."[41]

To the surprise of many, Cardinal Ernesto Corripio Ahumada, the primate of Mexico, also spoke out. Although he had been a colleague and friend at the Mexican Bishops Mutual Aid Union (UMAE) in the 1960s, he had hitherto kept a low profile in conflicts between Don Samuel and the government or the nuncio. But he had been angered by Prigione's efforts to split up the Mexico City archdiocese into several dioceses, a move that would also have meant that the archdiocese would probably no longer control the Basilica of Guadalupe. He had never supported Prigione in his negotiations with President Salinas for constitutional changes that would permit the establishment of diplomatic relations between Mexico and the Vatican State. He had been further offended when Prigione arranged with the Mexican government to give the Catholic Church as such juridic personality (not just its dioceses and other institutions), with Prigione — not the cardinal — identified as the official representative of the church in Mexico. As nuncio, he is simply the ambassador of the Vatican State.

❖

Nowhere was the support for Don Samuel so overwhelming as in his own diocese. An extraordinary session of the diocesan assembly consisting of men and women religious, laity, and priests, on November 2, eve of the bishop's sixty-ninth birthday, issued a two-page document expressing solidarity, respect, gratitude, and appreciation toward "Tatic" (a Tzeltal word meaning "great father"), the affectionate name by which the bishop is known in the diocese. To accuse him of errors, they said, is to accuse us also, as well as the thousands of men and women who implement the new evangelization in the diocese of San Cristóbal.

"We have always accepted responsibility for the consequences of being faithful to the Beatitudes and proclaiming the Resurrection. To be persecuted by the powerful is nothing new for us. The tortures and repressions and other injustices that the poor suffer fill us with indignation but also with courage to proclaim aloud that God wishes, not death, but life.

"How, we ask, can we remain silent when recently more than a thousand members of the Public Security forces broke up — with the use of force — a public and non-violent demonstration, wounding more than forty persons?...For some considerable time, and especially in the most recent years, attacks against the pastoral agents of the diocese have increased. They expelled a foreign priest, whose parish remains empty for lack of a replacement, falsely accusing him of being the intellectual agent of land seizures and of incitement of Guatemalan refugees to join the guerrillas. They illegally jailed another priest [Joel Padrón, pastor of Simojovel] for fifty days. Intense campaigns against Don Samuel were waged in the local and national press, radio and television. The authorities of most of the municipalities have misinformed the faithful Catholics, calumniating and maligning the bishop's work in defense of human rights. Some economically and politically powerful groups of the region have published on various occasions, especially during the pope's visit, defamatory and disrespectful leaflets. Some of these groups went so far as to propose killing their bishop and ours....

"We are filled with joy and hope at the support our Bishop "Tatic" has received. It cheers us to know that his evangelizing work has reached other parts of the country, of the continent, and of the world. It encourages us to persevere in prayer and in the proclamation of the gospel in these challenging and disturbing moments that Don Samuel has invited us to live as an hour of grace, a time of reflection, of conversion and of evangelization."

The bishop's birthday provided an opportunity for numerous visitors and hundreds of messages of support from all over the world. The clergy, religious, and laity filled the cathedral for a thanksgiving celebration. Archbishop (now Cardinal) Adolfo Suárez Rivera of Monterrey, head of the Conference of Mexican Bishops, announced in a press release that Don Samuel as "head of the diocese had been satisfactory for the episcopacy." Twenty thousand Catholic and Protestant indigenous of the diocese, assembled in the Representative Council of the Indigenous of the Chiapan highlands, sent Pope John Paul II their "humble petition that the bishop continue as head of the diocese."

At a press conference in Tuxtla Gutiérrez the following day (November 4), Don Samuel, speaking calmly and confidently, gave additional details about his October 26 meeting in Mexico City with Prigione. He said that the document sent from Rome asking for his resignation did not identify the group or groups who had accused him of pastoral errors. What it said, however, was similar to frequently repeated charges of Chiapan ranchers. Prigione told him that if these charges were well founded, he should change the pastoral practice of the diocese or perhaps voluntarily resign. He answered: "Many thanks, but I do not recognize myself in this letter; it appears that they are talking about a different situation and a different person. We will review the situation so that we can give an adequate response, because we are not isolated but in union with the universal church in which our stance is the same as that of many others."[42]

Don Samuel may have been confident as he spoke in Tuxtla Gutiérrez. And if the only issue were the rightness of his cause, he would have had good reason for his optimism. Unfortunately, that is not the only issue when one deals with either civil or ecclesiastical politics. And many of his friends feared that things might not go well for him as the year drew to its close. Then, unexpectedly, the New Year dawned with a cataclysm that altered in the bishop's favor major factors in the equation.

*Chapter 7*

# THE ZAPATISTA UPRISING

MEXICO'S President Salinas de Gortari had looked forward longingly to New Year's Day 1994. The North American Free Trade Agreement (NAFTA), the historic monument to his six years as president, would come into effect. It meant, he had said, that Mexico had become a First World country; it was moving into the twenty-first century.

Instead, in the first few hours of 1994, a military force, about the existence of which no whisper had ever appeared in the Mexican or international media, burst out of the Lacandon jungle and occupied San Cristóbal de Las Casas and six other cities and towns in the highlands of Chiapas. In San Cristóbal they cut phone lines, blocked roads, seized radio communications equipment, scattered municipal records, and released 179 prisoners from the jail. In his first communiqué, the mysterious, masked Subcomandante Marcos announced in the name of the Zapatista Army of National Liberation (EZLN) that NAFTA was the trigger that set off the explosion. It was, he said, "a death certificate for the indigenous peoples of Mexico."

For up to four days the Zapatistas held these communities until forced by massive attacks of the Mexican armed forces to withdraw to their bases in Lacandona. Meanwhile, Mexican government officials at both the state and national levels publicly and vociferously denounced the Catholic Church for fomenting the unrest. They particularly targeted the diocese

94

of San Cristóbal and its bishop. Their pastoral practices, they asserted, particularly their consciousness-raising techniques of evangelization, had excited the previously contented indigenous and thus encouraged the Zapatista mobilization. Spokespersons for the Chiapas state government charged that "liberation theology" priests and deacons in Ocosingo had allowed the Zapatistas to broadcast communiqués by means of a radio communications system of the diocese of San Cristóbal, a system that in fact did not exist. Elmer Setzler, who in early 1993 had replaced González as governor of Chiapas, focused on "the Catholic priests espousing liberation theology and their deacons" as the corrupters. In Mexico City the Televisa television network reported that Pablo Romo, the Dominican priest in charge of the human rights center of the diocese of San Cristóbal, was one of the military leaders of the Zapatistas. Undersecretary of the Interior Socorro Diaz joined the chorus with the assertion that members of religious orders were supporting the rebels.

While the army moved ahead with a build-up for a massive onslaught on the rebel base, politicians struggled frantically for a peaceful solution. Given the physical obstacles to a successful invasion of the Lacandon jungle, the low morale of the Mexican army, and that army's lack of training for jungle warfare, a military initiative might cause Mexico to become bogged down indefinitely in an inconclusive war. Were that to happen, the negative impact on the hoped-for infusion of foreign capital with the inauguration of NAFTA could be disastrous. In addition, the widespread expressions of admiration and even of support for the Zapatistas both throughout Mexico and abroad could translate into defeat for the government party, the PRI, in the presidential elections scheduled for August.

While seeking to cast the blame for the uprising on the bishop of San Cristóbal and the policies he had established in his diocese, the government made another astute political move. It attempted to show that neither the bishop nor the Zapatistas had a significant following in Chiapas. There were, it said, hundreds of organizations of the indigenous and campesinos in the Chiapan highlands that had not joined in the uprising. These organizations spoke for the people of Chiapas, not the rebels who had been deceived by foreign agitators and the liberation theology priests. Their failure to participate showed that the Zapatistas lacked a popular base.

The response of the organizations, which had reacted immediately to the uprising by starting to form a coalition that soon became a major player, the Chiapas State Council of Indigenous and Campesino Organizations (CEOIC), was not what the government wanted to hear. It is true, they said, that we do not approve of the recourse to armed force by the Zapatistas, but we support their objectives wholeheartedly. In that sense they speak for all of us.

The political sophistication of the Zapatista strategy had in fact been astonishing. The non-indigenous spokesperson for the indigenous of the Lacandon jungle (and as it soon became clear, for all the indigenous of Mexico), the mysterious, pipe-smoking Marcos, emphasized in the first communiqué that the armed protest was not exclusively on behalf of the indigenous but of all Mexicans who "have nothing, absolutely nothing, not a single roof, nor land, nor work, nor health, nor adequate food, nor education, nor the right to elect our representatives freely and democratically, nor independence from foreigners, nor justice for ourselves and our children."

It also soon became clear that this was a very unusual war. Its objective was not to seize power. The Zapatistas, with perhaps a thousand men and women in arms, could hold out in the jungle for a long time against the Mexican army's estimated two hundred thousand troops, but they had absolutely no offensive potential. They were an armed pressure group rather than a guerrilla army. The struggle was to be primarily a battle of ideas, a battle about human rights, the possibility of change. Its objective was to create a situation in which Mexicans could determine democratically their own future.

❖

To complicate the problems of the Mexican government, the United States quickly made it clear that its reaction was not the knee-jerk endorsement of the status quo against progressive reformers that had characterized its support of Central American military dictators during the Cold War. Already on January 6, U.S. Assistant Secretary of State for Latin America Alexander Watson set out the changed line. Chiapas, he stated publicly, demonstrates that "poverty, negligence, and the failure of governments to deal adequately with the concerns of the people can over time bring very serious consequences."

Faced with these realities, the government gave in. It not only called for dialogue and mediation to end the confrontation but agreed to the condition for discussions imposed by the Zapatistas, namely, that Don Samuel be the go-between.

The depiction of the bishop of San Cristóbal that appeared in the government-controlled media changed miraculously overnight. Forgotten — at least for the moment — was Samuel Ruiz, Zapatista leader, Pol Pot of Chiapas, intellectual mentor of the Revolution. In his place, Don Samuel, statesman, religious leader, envoy of peace, hailed alike by the government spokespersons and by Mexico's bishops.

An immediate casualty of the strategy was Don Samuel's long-time enemy, Patrocinio González Garrido, former governor of Chiapas. In January 1993 he had been promoted to the most important post after the presidency in the federal government, the Interior Secretariat which is responsible for law enforcement and the national security apparatus. Blamed for having failed to take preventive action against the Zapatista threat, of which the security forces had knowledge for nearly a year, he was forced to resign. His replacement was Jorge Carpizo, the attorney general and former human rights ombudsman. The choice of one identified with human rights was intended to assure public opinion that the government was responding positively to the charges of torturing and killing Zapatista prisoners being leveled against the army.

The politically important newly created post of Commissioner for Peace and Reconciliation in Chiapas was given to one of the few PRI politicians with a reputation for honesty, Manuel Camacho, the foreign minister and a former mayor of Mexico City. Camacho was not technically a representative of the Mexican government but the personal representative of President Salinas. Given the Mexican system, in which the president has very wide powers, the difference was not significant.

Camacho's first move was to seek the active support of the Catholic Church leaders. This was essential to starting negotiations with the Zapatistas, given that they had made it clear they would negotiate through the bishop of San Cristóbal. He arranged to meet at the offices of the Mexico City archdiocese with Archbishop Adolfo Suárez Rivera (Camacho's cousin and formerly a priest of the diocese of San Cristóbal), Cardinal Corripio, Bishop Ruiz, superiors of important religious orders, and the permanent board of the Mexican Bishops Conference (CEM). The meeting resulted in the creation by the bishops of a Commission of Reconciliation and Peace (CRP), composed of Ruiz and six other bishops. The inclusion of Ruiz represented a public expression of support, a major change of position for the Bishops Conference. Only a month earlier, most of the bishops had adopted a hands-off attitude when Prigione was urging Ruiz to resign.

Don Samuel's acceptance of the role of intermediary did not cause either him or his fellow workers to limit their activities on behalf of the indigenous. Father Gonzalo Ituarte, O.P., vicar general of the diocese, explained to a fact-finding delegation from the United States in early February the reasons, in the judgment of the diocese, for the Zapatista uprising.

"The real problem is that even with such a clear situation as we have here in Chiapas, of poverty, discrimination, and marginalization, nothing was ever done. Those who are really responsible for this war are the authorities and the wealthy landowners who control the local government. The indigenous people have been denied justice for five hundred years."[43]

Don Samuel was equally explicit. Here are typical comments he made about the same time. "During the negotiations for the NAFTA agreement, the law was changed so that the indigenous can sell their land. This was presented as a great improvement in the Constitution, but for the indigenous peoples the heart of their identity is the land. They will lose their identity with this new change....

"Chiapas is poor because of the unjust structures of an economic model that has systematically enriched a few people at the expense of the majority. The structural adjustment program, imposed on us by the current Mexican government to further integrate Mexico into the capitalist bloc of the north, only makes it easier for private interests to control the resources of the countryside.... The wealthy need two things to be able to continue this path of enrichment: privatization and NAFTA....

"The Zapatista uprising represents a questioning of the world economic system; the better the system functions, the greater the concentration of wealth. These events question that entire logic. It is a cry of challenge to the whole system."[44]

❖

Although government critics of the bishop had been silenced, the ranchers and businessmen of Chiapas kept up their attacks. In February, the Civic Front Against the Destabilizers called for a crusade against "the bishop and all those priests who profess the theology of liberation in the state of Chiapas." Although unsuccessful in its efforts to prevent the proposed discussions between the government and the Zapatistas, it continued to agitate. The intensity of the hatred is well conveyed by a demonstration in September 1994 outside La Merced Church in San Cristóbal. As the bishop arrived to say Mass, several hundred well-dressed men and women screamed insults and waved signs reading "Ruiz Antichrist," "Bishop of the Devil," "Go to Cuba." Seals placed on the doors of the church buildings read: "Fellow Catholics. Beginning today, this church and all those of the city will remain closed until Bishop Samuel Ruiz leaves the city, Chiapas, and Mexico. He is responsible for land takeovers and war in the region.... Pray and worship at home. God knows you are with him, and God is everywhere."[45]

As the stalemate in the Lacandon jungle dragged on through the spring and summer, the campaign of denigration expanded to reach all progressive elements in the church. Mexico City's *Summa* focused on the Jesuits, who had long been human rights activists at the national level. A financial daily newspaper headed by right-winger Jacobo Zabludovsky and rumored to have Opus Dei support, *Summa* is published by Televisa, the television chain owned by the Azcarraga family, one of the wealthiest and most powerful in Mexico. Marcos is a Jesuit, screamed *Summa* as part of a campaign to establish a link between PRD presidential candidate Cuautémoc Cárdenas and the progressive religious sectors. But, as a group of Jesuits charged in July, there was a further motive. The campaign, they said, was "orchestrated by right-wing groups in the general public and in the government" to force the Jesuits to withdraw from their commitment to social justice.

*Impacto,* a magazine that circulates widely all over Mexico, joined in the attack, accusing Jesuits in Chihuahua of supporting the Chihuahua Armed Command, a guerrilla group that existed only in *Impacto*'s imagination. Armed men raided Jesuit houses in Chiapas and in Morelos. Posters affixed to various Jesuit residences in Mexico City read: "In El Salvador thousands of indigenous died before the Jesuits who were responsible for their massacre. In Mexico, the Jesuits will die first." The posters were signed "Squads for the defense of the Catholic faith and peace in Mexico."[46] The campaign became so vicious that the Jesuits filed a libel action against *Summa*. But given the venality of the Mexican legal system, the likelihood that justice will be done is slight.[47]

Once the government had agreed to accept Don Samuel as mediator, the negotiations quickly got into high gear. Discussions opened in the cathedral of San Cristóbal — renamed for the occasion the "Cathedral of Peace" — on February 21. Observers from all parts of Mexico and many countries, organized by human rights and other non-governmental organizations, maintained a constant presence in the vicinity of the cathedral as a protection for the Zapatista representatives. Four hundred Mexican and foreign journalists attested to the importance of the occasion, the first time in history that a small, obscure group of rebels had in a few weeks been given de facto recognition as a social force by a sovereign government.

The Zapatista delegates, numbering nineteen, arrived under escort. Most were indigenous and wore their native dress. All used ski masks to conceal their identity. Twelve of them were members of the Zapatista political coordinating committee. The others, including Marcos, were military leaders. They carried with them a series of radical demands. The first step, they said, must be the creation of a true democracy in Mexico. That would mean that the president and state officials "who reached their positions of power through fraud" should resign, so that new elections could be held. Further demands were that the EZLN be recognized as a belligerent force, that NAFTA be revised, that indigenous languages be made official in their respective areas, that the indigenous be allowed to govern themselves and administer justice in their communities, and that the resources of Chiapas be used to create human living conditions for all its citizens.

Discussion of the thirty-four points presented by the Zapatistas continued for two weeks. The government replied to each point but for the most part in very general terms, at times not really addressing the issue raised. In response to the demands for democracy and resignation of elected officials, for example, it proposed a special session of Congress to discuss electoral reform. It also offered to enact a General Law for the Rights of Indigenous Communities that would take care of the numerous agrarian conflicts. On the day after the signing of a peace agreement, an amnesty law, both federal

and state, would protect the Zapatistas and free those imprisoned for having participated in the conflict. A new Chiapan
penal code would guarantee individual and political rights.
The government also promised significant community development programs in Chiapas: rural electrification, price
supports for agricultural products, childbirth clinics and day-
care centers with adequate food for children, and a general
program to end hunger and malnutrition. At least by impli-
cation, they recognized the legitimacy of the Zapatista social
demands.

Even before the discussions began, the Zapatistas had
made it clear that they had originally armed and trained, not
with the intention of starting an uprising but only to protect
themselves against the *guardias blancas* and *pistoleros* (death
squads) hired and controlled by the ranchers. They had seized
the six cities and towns on New Year's Day merely as a way
to dramatize the urgent need for change. But they would hold
on to their arms until the death squads had been demobilized
and disarmed and other major government commitments implemented. As a spokesperson told the press, "They have
always made promises, and they never have delivered. We
don't want them to trick us again. That is why we took up
weapons, and we won't turn them in for nothing."[48]

On March 2, the Zapatista delegates went back to their
base in the Lacandon jungle. The next step, they said, was
to ask their people to evaluate the government's offer. It was
not until June 10, that they announced the result of this process. Of the 64,712 people consulted, only 2 percent voted
to accept the offer. The vote for rejection was 98 percent. A
vote on renewing hostilities was equally decisive. Only 3 percent favored. The EZLN accordingly announced that, while
they rejected the government's proposals, they would not
break the cease-fire, nor would they disrupt the presidential
elections scheduled for August 21.

Reaction within the government party, the PRI, was mixed.
Public opinion had already been disturbed in March when the
presidential candidate for president, Luis Donaldo Colosio,

was assassinated. There were persistent rumors that hard-liners within the PRI itself, unhappy with the policies of Salinas and his hand-picked successor, were responsible; although convincing proofs were never adduced, neither has an explanation acceptable to the public been presented. The new PRI candidate for president, Ernesto Zedillo Ponce de León, responded to the EZLN rejection of the government offer by criticizing Manuel Camacho Solís, the government negotiator, and indicating that the only solution was a military one. Seeing himself undercut by his own people, Camacho Solís resigned as mediator. Don Samuel followed suit on the ground that there was no longer a mediating process, while insisting that he was always available as a go-between if called upon.

In spite of the stand of the PRI presidential candidate, hard-liner Zedillo, more cautious elements in the party opted against the use of force on the eve of elections. With perhaps a thousand Zapatistas armed in Lacandona and credible reports of groups arming themselves in at least seven other Mexican states, they decided the risks were too high. A military operation could bog down indefinitely in the jungle. A dangerously militant peasant movement could precipitate violence in many parts of the country.

❖

Although he had resigned as mediator, Don Samuel continued to work forcefully for a peaceful solution. His commitment to the justice of the Zapatista cause remained very clear, and he repeatedly formulated his view that what Mexico most needs is the development of civil society as "a historical subject" that will take effective control of the state structures and ensure that they function for the common good.

What does he mean by civil society? *La Señora Sociedad Civil* ("lady civil society") "is still something very vague in Mexico," he told a fact-finding delegation from the United States, on July 24, 1994. "It is for me professionals, civil movements, political parties, non-governmental organizations, people who work in government departments not as administrators but as employees, then the baptized Christians of many kinds, the universities. It's the people of Mexico. Voting is not the only function of the people. The life of the nation goes far beyond voting. It goes beyond political parties, so that it can demand that whoever wins the elections develop a society that leads toward an authentic transition in the direction of democracy.

"This civil society is being manipulated now by many interests. The cattle ranchers, for example, are fearful that a civil society leading to more just structures will force them to give up some of their land. What drives political parties is a commitment, not to promote civil society for its own sake, but to win. The PRI, now identical with the state, does not want to give up power. It makes concessions only to retain its grip. NAFTA is also putting pressure on the PRI government, because the United States and Canada want to maintain NAFTA. Civil society is thus under many pressures as it attempts to establish itself as the ultimate guide of the state."[49]

The bishop's clear statement of his vision for Mexico is particularly important because it was made just some weeks after the Zapatistas had issued in mid-June their Second Declaration from the Lacandon Jungle.[50] That declaration called for "a national dialogue with the theme of democracy, freedom, and justice," and it invited representatives of every ejido, settlement, school, and factory of every state of Mexico to a National Democratic Convention to be held in a Zapatista community on a future date. They envisaged the convention, they said, as leading to a transitional government, the enactment of a new constitution, and elections.

The Zapatistas repeated what they had stated on many occasions, namely, that they did not want to seize power by force of arms. What they hoped for was a massive alliance of "workers, squatters, housewives, students, teachers, intellectuals, writers, and all of those who with dignity resist with us." The similarity to Don Samuel's understanding of civil society is striking.

Some confusion, nevertheless, was caused by different wording in the various communiqués the Zapatistas issued as they promoted the idea of the meeting. In one, they invited civil society to unite in order to define the country's political road. In another, they said the convention would be held in territory they controlled, and its purpose would be to overthrow the government of Salinas and produce a new constitution. The different statements of purpose brought conflicting reactions from groups that had planned to participate. Some said they would not go because they suspected that the Zapatista initiative was simply designed to broaden their base. Others said they believed they should attend, even if not certain about the intentions of the Zapatistas, because they felt it important to have input on behalf of a peaceful solution. Yet other groups, identified with the extreme left and some even with terrorists, said they definitely wanted to come. To resolve the confusion, the Zapatistas issued yet another statement. Movements that were not pacifist, they said, would not be allowed to participate. The purpose of the convention was to invite civil society to seek a political solution, not a military one, to Mexico's problems.

❖

The situation had by now reached comic-opera proportions. The Zapatista tail was apparently wagging the Mexican government dog. How long can this go on? the amazed and amused Mexican and world observers asked. Surely the government could not allow a rebel group to function as an independent state within its territory. Yet it did, and that fact surely demonstrates both its internal dissensions and its awareness of the weakness of its claim to legitimacy.

The convention was held in Aguascalientes, in Zapatista-controlled territory, August 6–9, 1994. It was an extraordinary organizational and logistical feat. Delegates and observers to the number of six thousand had to be accommodated in a location with none of the normal services of civilized society. Six hundred Zapatistas built the town of Aguascalientes in a month. The name was symbolic. Aguascalientes was the site of the first Constitutional Convention attended by Emiliano Zapata in 1914, a convention that led to the 1917 Constitution and the legislative recognition of *ejido* land ownership.

Ready for the visitors was an amphitheater with wooden benches for eight thousand people, a clinic, a library with more than three thousand volumes, long lines of latrines for men and women, kitchens, potable drinking water, a press building with electricity, and outlets for computers.

Represented were hundreds of indigenous and peasant organizations, movements of the urban poor and the working class, women, labor, students, artists, musicians, intellectuals, teachers, political parties, gay men and lesbians, ecologists, human rights activists, people from all parts of Mexico and as far away as China, New Zealand, Australia, France, and South Africa.

The convention produced no surprises. It reaffirmed the original Declaration of the Lacandon Jungle demanding work, land, housing, food, health, education, independence, liberty, democracy, justice, and peace. It called for the dismantling of the PRI, which it described as the party of the state, and also the dismantling of national security apparatuses and police forces that act outside the law. And it proposed a special convention to write a new constitution that would reinstate land distribution, define indigenous autonomy, and allow a democratic political culture to emerge.

Although some delegates lobbied hard for an endorsement of Cuautémoc Cárdenas, presidential candidate of the Democratic Republican Party (PRD), the convention refused to issue one. Apparently Marcos felt that to endorse any candidate would contradict the Zapatista commitment not to seek for itself political power. It would seem, however, that Marcos hoped for a Cárdenas victory, since his defeat in the elections the following month was a blow to the Zapatista cause.

There remains some mystery as to the Marcos/Cárdenas relationship. Marcos had snubbed Cárdenas shortly before the convention in a speech he made during a campaign visit by Cárdenas to Zapatista territory. Marcos did, however, use the convention to move forward his idea of recognizing civil society as the basis for a democratic state. The Zapatistas put their army at the disposition of the convention and committed themselves not to open hostilities again on their own. To declare war, they said, is a decision that must be made by civil society. In this way they have, at least symbolically, shared leadership with the broader Mexican society outside Chiapas.

The redefinition of democracy as active participation of civil society in its own governance had profound ideological significance. It is a clear rejection of the limited democracy, the right to cast a vote for one of two parties, each dominated by vested interests, that today's capitalist system would impose on all poor countries. It requires social movements of all kinds, stretching up from the very bases, to maintain an ongoing involvement in the functioning of national and local political institutions. It is a transfer to civil society of the structures that Don Samuel has created for his diocese. He would be the last to take credit, but it is surely more than coincidental that it is precisely in his diocese that this revolutionary approach to government has emerged.

## Chapter 8

# ROME VS. SAN CRISTÓBAL

THE DECISION of the Mexican government in early January 1994 to accept Don Samuel as go-between in its negotiations with the Zapatistas forced a tactical change in the scheme of those elements in the Vatican that wanted to get rid of him. Papal Nuncio Prigione, who had urged him to resign, insisting that such was the pope's wish, suspended his activities, at least in public. He had little choice. Patrocinio González Garrido, his friend and the bishop's enemy, was out of favor, having lost his job as secretary of the interior for failing to evaluate correctly the military strength of the EZLN and to take appropriate defense measures. In addition, although Prigione had always asserted that the Vatican's problems and his own problems with Don Samuel had nothing to do with Mexican politics, it was always clear that his real motive in seeking to oust Don Samuel was to curry favor with the government. For the moment, at least, the government wanted to hold on to the bishop of San Cristóbal.

For as long as that situation continued, consequently, Don Samuel was well protected against Vatican action. Few thought in early 1994 that the government/Zapatista stalemate could continue for more than a few months at the outside. But nearly two years later, the unstable equilibrium still held, evidence of the extraordinary support of public opinion in Mexico and worldwide for the Zapatistas and of the government's awareness of the fragility of its own legitimacy.

There was consequently no further public statement during 1994 concerning Rome's canonical investigation. But, as later emerged, it was not abandoned. Quite apart from Prigione's intentions and objectives, Don Samuel has raised issues that are of deep concern both to Cardinal Ratzinger as head of the Vatican watchdog on orthodoxy and to Pope John Paul II and his understanding of authority in the church.

❖

The account of the radical transformation of the diocese of San Cristóbal under the leadership of Don Samuel Ruiz that has already been given makes it clear that he has come to embrace and inculcate a certain ecclesiology, a certain understanding of what is the function of the church and how it should perform this function.

In his own words, already quoted, he believes in a church that is inculturated. Rome does indeed accord lip service to the concept. Given the emphasis placed by Vatican Council II on the need for the church to adapt to cultures other than European, as well as confirmatory statements in many official church documents, it could hardly do otherwise. But its understanding of what is involved is very different from Don Samuel's. As an observer commented during the 1994 African Synod in Rome, inculturation for John Paul II means an African dance at the Offering of the Gifts during the celebration of the Eucharist.

What does it mean for Don Samuel? A document of CELAM's Department of Missions, drafted by bishops of dioceses that contain considerable numbers of indigenous, provides the outlines. Evangelization, they say, must respect the cultural identity of each community. Following the guidelines of Paul VI's *Evangelii Nuntiandi* and of the Puebla 1979 meeting of the Latin American bishops, it should work to liberate all indigenous communities and recognize indigenous nationalities in all countries. It should also seek to establish autochthonous churches, thereby creating a new image of the Latin American church as pluricultural.

"Just as the apostles did not found a church at the start of evangelization, but rather by their missions caused a particular church to come into existence, so the church of our continent should favor the birth of particular indigenous churches, each with an autochthonous hierarchy and organization, with a theology, a liturgy, and an ecclesial manner adapted to their own culture and religious expression, in communion with the other particular churches, above all and basically with Peter. In this way, the authenticity and catholicity of a church incarnated in all cultures can best be manifested on our continent."[51]

The document insists on urgency. "In this historic hour for Latin America we hear the cry of the indigenous peoples rising from the four cardinal points of the continent. It is a cry that demands recognition and guarantees of their inalienable right to the ownership of the land. For these peoples, the land is not just a geographic territory or a means of reproduction; it is in the first place and above all a religious space with which they maintain their mystical relations, the place of their myths, of their history, of their celebrations and their fiestas; in a word, the place of their hope and their identity. We also hear the cry of the indigenous peoples demanding self-determination. And we are moved by the cry of their assassinated leaders, of their martyrs who worked to organize their peoples and build an alliance of the oppressed."

The already mentioned pastoral plan adopted at a general assembly of the diocese in 1986 shows both how far this concept of inculturation had already been put into practice and how ready were the pastoral agents to continue to move. It called for a critical evaluation of the cultures. The goal of the professional pastoral agents, it said, should be to insert themselves in the culture of the people, learning their languages and their history and encouraging their cultural expressions. They should share ecclesial responsibility with the laity, creating mechanisms for joint decision-making. The people should not have to come to the church structures; rather, pastoral agents and people should together create structures that enable all to participate.

"We all know that it is necessary to look critically at the world to which the call of the Lord is addressed and in which our action takes place. Only thus can we discover the riches given by the Father to his children even before our humble proclamation of the Good News. . . . Proper knowledge of our world will similarly help us to understand the many others whose efforts are also helping to build the Kingdom, whether from the perspective of a legitimate autonomy of the action of the laity in the church, or from the action of those who, perhaps without a clear understanding of God's saving plan, still envisage it in some way and make their commitment for the poor, who are the privileged hearers of the gospel."[52]

Diocesan pastoral teams maintain an ongoing examination of the results of their initiatives. A typical progress report speaks of the constant temptation of a church coming from a powerful culture to impose its values on weaker people in the name of spreading the gospel. It insists that top priority be given to incarnation in the indigenous cultures so that the gospel can be announced from within. Indigenous ministries must be developed in order to build an autochthonous church, especially the *tuhuneletic*. This Mayan word is the title of a traditional office in the communities. The *tuhuneletic* ("servants") carry out various social tasks, and the diocese uses the same word to describe what it calls "pre-deacons," of whom there are now more than four hundred in 2,608 communities. Other traditional offices are those of leaders, major-domos, and captains, and efforts are being made to incorporate all of these into the church structures, leading to the ordination of those selected as subdeacons, deacons, and priests (see chapter 11). The report notes that this development confronts the roadblock of current church legislation. Although the document does not specify, probably the biggest obstacle is imposed celibacy.

The initiative for the *tuhuneletic* came from the catechists themselves. Following the religious traditions of the indigenous, the community selects a respected member already known for community service as a candidate for a permanent diaconate, with power to administer sacraments and preside over traditional indigenous rituals. Since the mid-1970s, Don Samuel has been ordaining the *tuhuneletic*.

❖

In his account of his stewardship in the already mentioned pastoral letter on the occasion of the papal visit in August 1993, Don Samuel dealt at length with his understanding of and implementation of inculturation. Although he knows he may be providing ammunition to the nuncio and reactionaries in Rome, he is very forthcoming about what he is doing and why.

The economic and social processes of contemporary neoliberalism, he noted as he attacked the issue, seem to seek to eliminate the diversity of peoples as an obstruction in the way of attaining its objectives. Given that situation, there is an extreme urgency to establish an autochthonous church that has developed through its own historical, social, cultural, religious, and faith processes. The communitarian structures and a lifestyle of solidarity and service in the indigenous Mayan cultures favor and facilitate the reception of the Good News, and this feeds hope that before long we can have many indigenous priests.

The indigenous and campesino communities, the bishop notes, have already taken significant steps toward becoming the subjects of their own history and no longer the objects of decisions made by others. A growing consciousness of dignity that has been fed by evangelical values has contributed to this advance. The people are occupying the space that is theirs by right in the church and therefore also in history.

A very clear statement of the principles on which the diocesan pastoral approach is based follows. "Every pastoral action will be legitimate if it is liberating, if it respects the lawful decisions of the people of God, joining their journey, favoring the weakest, and taking their culture, religiosity, and needs into account."

Why does this approach to evangelization disturb the Rome of Ratzinger and John Paul II? At the conscious level, because it is based on an ecclesiology, an understanding of how the church is constituted and how it should function, that they reject. Rejection at the conscious level is probably reinforced by a subconscious sense that this kind of de-Europeanized church would cease to look to Rome to resolve its routine problems.

The philosophical presumptions underlying these two understandings of what church is all about were identified by José Comblin in an analysis of a preparatory document for the 1992 Conference of the Latin American Bishops.[53] A Belgian who since the 1950s has worked in Chile and Brazil, Father Comblin was a major architect of the historic Medellín documents, which applied the teachings of the Second Vatican Council to Latin America. The document he analyzed was part of an ambitious effort by the Roman curia, with the approval of Ratzinger and the pope, to end the partial autonomy acquired by the Latin American bishops as a result of the Vatican Council. It sought to do so by imposing a theology new to Latin America: neotraditionalism. This would mean, not just taking the church back to pre–Vatican II, but to pre–Vatican I (1870).

Nineteenth-century traditionalism, Comblin wrote, was inspired by philosophers and proto-sociologists who led the criticism of the French Revolution. They focused on ideas, not objective reality, to explain events. For them, the Revolution was caused, not by the hunger of the masses, but by the philosophy of the Enlightenment.

Professional theologians accepted this sociological analysis. They had already rejected the French Revolution and the society that resulted from it. The excesses of that revolution they ascribed to the inability of the masses to control themselves. In an interpretation of the Fall close to that of John Calvin, they decided that human reason had been so impaired by original sin that humans were incapable of reaching truth by their own unaided powers. They needed the benefit of revelation.

All peoples are presented in this interpretation as having some level of revelation to help them, namely, the original revelation God gave to Adam when they walked and chatted together in the Garden of Eden. The People of the Book have a further level of revelation given to Moses on Mount Sinai. But the fullness of revelation is available only to Christians, and that through the church founded by Christ and charged with the duty of feeding his lambs. Such an understanding of human existence and of the church as enjoying a monopoly of truth is obviously incompatible with Don Samuel's understanding of a church that learns from those it seeks to evangelize.

The documents analyzed by Comblin, which were drafted by or under the influence of the Roman curia in the hope of deflecting the Latin American church from its interpretation of the Second Vatican Council, reveal the problems faced by Don Samuel and other bishops who work for a radical inculturation of the church in the indigenous peoples of Latin America. They assume a social integration in Latin America that has never occurred, ignoring the continuous revolts of the indigenous for five hundred years, the struggles of slaves, and the later struggles of peasants and workers. The continuing liberation struggles, which Don Samuel and his associates support, are for them factors of disintegration, destructive of the social fabric.

This misreading of history matches a particular understanding of authority in the church and in society. It thinks of medieval Europe, ruled by a concert of popes, emperors, and kings, as the ideal Christian society. They were the source of all good. Everything else was disruptive. In all logic, Don Samuel's efforts to democratize the church in his diocese are a grave error for this school of thought. The enthusiastic response of the indigenous to his initiatives shows how grave the danger is, how important it is to act decisively.

# Chapter 9

# RUIZ A MARXIST?

D ON SAMUEL has also become caught up in the contro-
versy within the church about liberation theology. The
name was first given in the late 1960s to a theology that
had been elaborated by Latin Americans influenced by the
Vatican Council. It was the first non-European theological
system developed by Christian thinkers in more than a thousand years. One novelty was the cooperation of Catholics and
Protestants in the effort, an indication that Latin American
Christians were transcending the sixteenth-century Reforma-
tion, which after all was for them merely another part of
the baggage imported to their continent by the European
invaders.

A more important distinguishing feature was its use of the
social sciences to define the reality of each existential situation before looking to the Scriptures for guidance on how
to respond. All earlier theologies had begun from first principles — that often owed more to Aristotle than to the gospel —
using their theoretical constructs to determine how to react to
the perceived needs of the moment.

Also integral to liberation theology is its focus on the preferential option for the poor. What this means is that the
Christian message must be formulated in terms that promote
the liberation of the oppressed masses.

The liberation theologians incorporated into a scientific

body of thought and reflection about the meaning of God and of human existence (which is what theology is) the formula developed in popular youth movements of northwestern Europe by Canon (later Cardinal) Cardijn): See-Judge-Act. One first analyzes a situation, then reflects on it in the light of the Scriptures, and finally decides upon the answer that God speaking through the Scriptures calls for.

While European theologians in the fourth quarter of the twentieth century might be agitated about the "death of God," papal infallibility, or the threat of institutionalized atheism, one who looked at Latin America identified other pressing realities, just as Don Samuel did in Chiapas in the early 1960s. The analysis of that reality by the first liberation theologians quickly produced a consensus that extreme and growing poverty was the overriding issue, and that this poverty was not a natural condition; the poor have been made poor by others at the personal, societal, national, and international levels. Their poverty was the inevitable result of systemic structures that impoverished Latin America — and the rest of the Third World — for the benefit of the powerful industrial countries who control social structures.

The theological breakthrough followed, and could not have occurred without, a breakthrough at the level of the human sciences. Argentine economist Raúl Prebisch had told the first meeting of the UN Commission on Trade and Development (UNCTAD) in 1964 that the "periphery" must consistently sell its raw materials for less while the manufacturing products of the "center" are sold for consistently higher prices, a structural and growing disequilibrium. His analysis substituted for the trickle-down theory of developmentalism, which had provided the justification for the Alliance for Progress, a dependency theory that proclaims the poverty of the peripheral countries to be the result of systematic exploitation by the dominant countries of the center.

The bishops of Latin America at Medellín, Colombia, in 1968 formally accepted this analysis and committed the church to a preferential option for the poor. Their meeting at Puebla, Mexico, in 1979, reaffirmed this stand. The new concern for the poor expressed itself in support of grassroots organizations in the form of Christian base communities, which helped the poor to become subjects of their own history and in which they discovered for themselves that salvation comes not from benevolent outsiders but from their own efforts.

All of this represented, of course, a radical change in the official relations between the Latin American bishops and the oligarchies who control civil society. The reaction of the latter was not long in coming, especially in the countries controlled in the 1960s and later by military dictatorships. Many bishops yielded to the pressures and continue the traditional support of the powerful. Many did not and have paid the price, which in some instances — as in that of Archbishop Oscar Arnulfo Romero of San Salvador — meant death. Important thinkers were driven by military dictators into exile. They included Paulo Freire, José Comblin, Hugo Assmann, Franz Hinkelammert, and Enrique Dussel.

The United States, recognizing the threat to the social order that it believed protected its interests, was not slow to intervene. Nelson Rockefeller in 1969 warned that the United States could no longer count on the automatic support of the Latin American church. The Santa Fe Declarations, which offered policy guidance to President Reagan, went further. They called for active U.S. opposition to liberation theology.

Pope Pius XI in *Quadragesimo Anno* (1931) had already reflected the essential elements both of the Marxist analysis and of the Marxist critique of capitalism, and his lead has been followed in all subsequent papal documents dealing with the social order. But it was not until Paul VI's *Octogesima Adveniens*, commemorating the eightieth anniversary in 1971 of Leo XIII's *Rerum Novarum*, that a pope explicitly approved the use of what Paul called "a more attenuated form of Marxism." It was an approval hedged with reservations, but it agreed that the Marxist analysis could be "a working tool" that provided "a certitude preliminary to action."

Three years later, the same pope set up the International Theological Commission to look more deeply into liberation theology. Its report issued in 1976 recognized that theological explanations of poverty and oppression of the poor required sociological theories in order to analyze the "Cry of the People" calmly and objectively. It again warned of dangers in using sociological theories, including those of Marxism-Leninism, and urged theologians to keep these dangers in mind.

Liberation theologians do indeed make class analysis a central and indisputable element for understanding the social situation, as Marx did. Its use is at least implicit in the theory of dependence, a theory that rests on the general methodological assumption that there exist enduring social structures that limit the range of possibilities at a given historical moment. It is properly described as neo-Marxist, formulated not by Marx himself but by the research tradition he inaugurated.

These theologians stress the major impact on political and cultural developments of the interests of the class that owns the means of production. They similarly repeat Marx's critique of the fetishism of capitalism. And they are emotionally close to Marx's "materialism" in their insistence that salvation is not just a matter of an afterlife but the proper goal of all human endeavor on earth.

They are very specific, however, in their rejection of Marx's atheism. In agreement with many Eurocommunists, they insist it is not an integral part of his system. Their widespread use of Marxist terminology and concepts simply reflects the fact that Marx has become as much a part of the intellectual context of Latin America as is Freud of that of the United States.

❖

Liberation theologians, however, are not the only ones whose thinking Marx has influenced. In his 1981 encyclical *La-*

*borem exercens,* Pope John Paul II used a new conceptual framework clearly inspired by Marx when discussing such concepts as "class," "work in the objective sense," "work in the subjective sense," "priority of labor over capital," and "capacity for work."

The pope's adoption of Marxist categories should logically have put an end to the discussion, but nothing of the sort has happened. The reason may be that he has absorbed these categories unconsciously from the intellectual culture in which he was socialized and does not realize that he is using them. Perhaps he is also influenced by the attitudes of the United States, whose policies over a very wide range he has faithfully paralleled. Whatever the reason, John Paul continues to warn liberation theologians of the dangers of Marxist thought.

Shortly after he was appointed head of the Vatican watchdog on orthodoxy, the Congregation for the Doctrine of the Faith, Cardinal Joseph Ratzinger took the lead in the struggle to delegitimate liberation theology. In 1984, he published an article in Peru, Italy, and Germany, in which he characterized liberation theology as incompatible with the Christian faith, singling out Gustavo Gutiérrez and Leonardo Boff for his severest criticisms.[54] The first publication was anonymous, but the others identified Ratzinger as the author.

The article was followed up the same year by a formal statement from the Congregation for the Doctrine of the Faith, *Instruction on Certain Aspects of the "Theology of Liberation."* It not only condemned every theology that "tries to adopt" the Marxist analysis, but challenged the dependency theory. While recognizing the fact of extreme poverty, oppression, and "a mockery of elementary human rights" in many parts of Latin America, it blamed these conditions, not on social structures, but on the licentiousness and downright evil of individuals who played certain roles in those structures. The logic of the exposition was that the oppressed must suffer patiently until their oppressors are converted.

Ratzinger here touches on an issue that is central to the entire conflict. Liberation theology identifies the oppressors as a class who monopolize power and the oppressed as a class who have to organize in order to obtain balancing power and become subjects of their own history. This is quite different from papal social teaching, which rejects the idea of asymmetrical powers that must be corrected before the oppressed can escape their often intolerable condition. According to papal social teaching, change can come only with the conversion of the wicked individuals, which means by consensus and agreement. The wealthy understandably welcome this approach. It would bring the Latin American church back to its traditional role of working hand-in-hand with the landowners to provide stability.

The Ratzinger document ended by saying it had dealt mostly with the negative aspects of liberation theology and that a later statement would evaluate the positive aspects. Issued in 1986, the second statement had something to say about a multitude of issues, from ecology to human rights to soteriological liberation. And it ended up by insisting that all the condemnations in the earlier document remained valid.[55]

The United States business interests, which — as already noted — feared all social change in Latin America, welcomed this support for their position. The Institute on Religion and Democracy, the Heritage Foundation, and the American Enterprise Institute, all conservative think tanks, became the major — or at least the most visible — implementers of the policy of actively opposing and countering liberation theology. Such right-wing groups in Mexico as the strongly anti-communist and fascist-leaning Pro-Vida joined suit, and they have been extremely successful in associating liberation theology and Marxism in the public mind.

❖

Don Samuel has not become involved in the theoretical discussion about liberation theology. He dismisses questions by saying that it was not an a priori commitment to this or any other theology but rather an independent analysis of the objective situation that persuaded the diocese to embark on its innovative pastoral program. At the same time, he makes no secret of his support for the progressive Latin American church of which liberation theology is a characteristic.

He came in for a lot of criticism from conservative Mexican bishops for his participation, along with two other Mexican bishops, Sergio Méndez Arceo of Cuernavaca and José Pablo Rovalo of Zacatecas, in a pastoral congress in Riobamba, Ecuador, diocese of Bishop Leónidas Proaño. At the August 1974 meeting were some twenty bishops, four from the United States, the others from all parts of Latin America. With them were thirty theologians, some of the most prestigious of Latin America.

The proceedings were abruptly ended on the fourth day when forty armed policemen burst into the conference room. Without time to collect any clothes, the bishops and theologians were bundled into a police bus, eighty people including armed guards in a vehicle designed for fifty. "For the first time in my life I knew what it was like to have a rifle shoved in my back," Venezuelan Bishop Mariano Parra León commented later. They were driven three hours through the mountains to Quito, where they were dumped in jail.

Ecuador's Interior Minister Javier Manrique told the international press that "friendly governments" had warned that the Riobamba conspirators were "subversive communists plotting the government's overthrow." It took some days to sort out the entire mess, of which the most serious result was a heart attack suffered by Bishop Parra León. But there were repercussions back home for the Mexican participants. Several bishops criticized them for having been involved, and a Mexican theologian on the staff of CELAM wrote a report that came close to justifying the Ecuadorian military's application of the "doctrine of national security."

Since 1985 Don Samuel has been a leading figure in the "Oscar Arnulfo Romero" International Christian Secretariat of Solidarity with the Peoples of Latin America (SICSAL), and was host in 1991 to its an annual commemoration of the martyred archbishop of San Salvador. When SICSAL founder

Bishop Méndez Arceo of Cuernavaca died the following year, he accepted the presidency of the organization.

All these activities are, of course, perfectly legitimate. But they do provide ammunition to his enemies in the Mexican and Chiapan power structures. Given the clearly demonstrated anxiety of the Vatican to improve its relations with the Mexican government and the parallel interest of major figures in the Roman curia in opposing innovations in the Latin American church, they could be misinterpreted to the detriment of the bishop of San Cristóbal. As the year 1993 drew to its close, many feared that his days were numbered, that he would either be forced to resign or be neutralized in his diocese by the imposition of a coadjutor with overriding powers.

The unanticipated entrance of the Zapatistas into the political life of Mexico brought relief to Don Samuel. As long as the stalemate continues in the Lacandon jungle, he continues to be the essential liaison for the Mexican government, and the Vatican is most unlikely to touch him. Its charges of grave doctrinal, pastoral, and administrative errors have, nevertheless, not been withdrawn. The case stands suspended, not closed.

# Chapter 10

# CHALLENGING THE *CACIQUES*

⟦▥▥▥⟧ ⟦▥▥▥⟧ ⟦▥▥▥⟧

D URING the entire period since Don Samuel arrived in San Cristóbal the church has been involved in a conflict in the municipality of Chamula that has been referred to many times in earlier chapters. That conflict has been used in various ways by both ecclesiastical and civil enemies of the bishop to malign him. In the media the conflict is often presented as resulting from the persecution of Protestants by Catholics, with the insinuation that the bishop and his pastoral agents approve of or connive with such discrimination and violation of human rights.

The reality is very different. The situation merits examination, not only to establish the truth, but to illustrate how sensitive Don Samuel is in his dealings with indigenous communities and how firmly he defends the human rights of Protestants no less than those of his own constituents.

The story of Chamula also throws light on many aspects of the history of the indigenous. During the nineteenth century, Conservatives and Liberals vied for control of their villages, the Liberals seeking to ban the Catholic Church and have unchallenged free access to their land and labor, the Conservatives wanting the priests to continue to administer the communities. When the former were in power, they told the people they were no longer obligated to pay the priests and could conduct religious services as they saw fit.

123

When the Conservatives regained control, the priest would come with them and demand back pay. One such priest in particular is remembered for his insistence on his rights. Miguel Martínez in 1865 refused to say Mass until they paid up, whipped officials who challenged him, and looted the coffers of the Maya religious societies. In this conflictive context, the traditional religions acquired greater respectability and open observance, resulting in a high level of intermingling of traditional pre-Christian rites and practices with Catholicism.

Chamula is the largest of twenty-five indigenous municipalities in the Chiapan highlands, an area of 140 square miles with a population of over a hundred thousand. The Chamulans pride themselves on their independence, and they make their own laws. While they welcome tourists, they do not hesitate to jail them if they transgress the regulations enacted by the municipality.

❖

In the rest of Mexico, the Liberals won the Revolution of 1910. In Chiapas, the Conservatives retained power, but when the Catholic Church was outlawed, the priests were replaced as administrators of the indigenous municipalities by *ladino* labor contractors (*enganchadores*). Lázaro Cárdenas, however, when president of Mexico in the 1930s, decided to break the power of the *enganchadores* by organizing a union of farm workers. Years of armed conflict followed before the indigenous union emerged as the victor, its leaders now developed into *caciques* ("bosses"), who have since ruled Chamula. In return for a guaranteed support of the PRI in elections, they were placed in charge of all government programs. Chamula had long been without a resident priest, and this enabled the *caciques* to gain control of all the religious associations (*cargos*). A priest had come from time to time to baptize, the only Catholic ceremony in which most Chamulans were interested.

A new source of conflict came to Chamula in the early

1950s with the arrival of a Presbyterian missionary employed by the Summer Institute of Linguistics. There he did bilingual work for the Institute, whose formal role was to translate the Bible into indigenous languages, while quietly proselytizing on the side, and in due course he made some converts in small villages on the eastern edge of the municipality of Chamula. They were not many in number, but the *caciques* soon recognized them as a threat. They were critical of the "superstitions" that formed an important part of the worship services in what was called a "Catholic" church, although the building was owned by the municipality and operated without a resident priest. Not less threatening was the refusal of the Protestants to go into debt for the compulsory purchase of alcohol, soft drinks, fireworks, and candles for religious festivals. This major source of income to the *caciques* was also the hook by which they kept the farm workers in debt bondage.

The first Protestants were Presbyterian. Later, other missionaries, mostly Seventh-day Adventists, made converts in villages located within the municipal boundaries of Chamula. Their lifestyle was equally objectionable to the *caciques*, since their beliefs were completely at variance with the *costumbre*, the customs and religious rites that gave the *caciques* their economic and social privileges.

Expelled from Chamula in 1968, a group of Protestants established themselves in a squatter village on the edge of San Cristóbal. Life was not easy for them in a city that was notoriously hostile to the indigenous. The Institute of Linguistics missionaries, however, helped them to adjust and found them jobs in the market. Thanks to their connections with Chamulans coming in to San Cristóbal to sell their handicrafts, they prospered.

❖

In the mid-1960s, the new bishop of San Cristóbal, Samuel Ruiz, sent a priest to live in Chamula. Leopoldo ("Padre Polo") Hernández took the job seriously, but his every initiative brought him into conflict with the *caciques*. He started a credit union that created competition with their loan business. When he built chapels in villages on the east edge of town, they were burned down because they threatened to break the religious monopoly of the center. Rumors were spread that Padre Polo was having trysts with indigenous women in the mountains, his automobile tires were slashed, and he was forced to leave.

Padre Polo had, however, gained many sympathizers in the villages that were part of the municipality and that resented the monopoly of the *caciques* of the center. As the 1973 municipal elections approached, he organized a candidature of the conservative Party of National Action (PAN). It was widely believed that they won the elections, but the *caciques* — helped by the PRI state machine — were declared the winners.

As punishment for their challenge to the *caciques* several hundred members of the opposition were loaded into trucks and dumped outside the municipality. Within weeks they had crept back home, but the next year they were again arrested and lodged in the Chamula jail, where some of them were beaten. The National Indigenous Institute (INI), a government body, intervened on their behalf. Fearing for their lives, it moved them to San Cristóbal where they joined the Protestants who had established themselves there six years earlier.

The expulsion of Padre Polo and his supporters ended the official presence of the Catholic Church in Chamula. The *caciques* brought in as pastor a minister of the Mexican Orthodox Church. This is a breakaway group from the Mexican Catholic Church. It is not related in any way with Eastern Orthodoxy. Married with children, the pastor was a *ladino*, a one-time Catholic seminarian. He baptized children and performed marriage ceremonies. He also celebrated the Eucharist, using tortillas and the locally distilled liquor known as *pox*, which is a major source of income to the *caciques* because of its important role in their fiestas.

In the 1970s and early 1980s, the expulsions continued, to a total of some fifteen thousand. Most of those expelled were Protestants, but some were Catholics who opposed the *caciques*. Don Samuel has repeatedly protested the human rights violations involved and has consistently helped the victims without regard to their religious affiliation. Meanwhile, the bishop continued to negotiate for the return of a priest to Chamula, and finally in August 1994, after the Orthodox Catholic pastor had left, he reached an agreement with the municipality. The new pastor is Gustavo López, and he will be accompanied in all liturgical ceremonies by a priest from the municipality of Bochil who is a Tzotzil.

Also in 1994, groups of expelled Chamulans decided they would follow the example of the Guatemalan refugees, who over enormous obstacles were returning from more than a decade of exile in Mexico to their homeland. During the period preceding the presidential elections in August, when the state authorities were anxious to minimize friction, several hundred did in fact resettle in their former villages. While they succeeded in reestablishing themselves, tension continues. In one outbreak of violence in the fall of 1994, three of the returnees were killed. And in a separate incident in December of that year, reported by the diocesan Human Rights Commission, eleven Catholics were expelled and their property seized. The municipal authorities charged that they had become Protestants, meaning — presumably — that they had refused to participate in the fiestas that constitute a major source of income for the *caciques*.

Arturo Farela Gutiérrez, president of the National Confraternity of Christian Evangelical Churches of Mexico, agrees with the diocese of San Cristóbal that the conflict in Chamula is not one between Catholics and Protestants. Those responsible for the violence in Chamula, he says, are the state governor, the local PRI, and the *caciques* placed in power and kept in power by the PRI. The religion of Chamula is the Catholic Orthodox group, which is manipulated by the PRI authorities and which does not even respect the Roman

Catholic Church headed by Bishop Samuel Ruiz. The only solution is for the federal government to intervene and ensure
that the constitutional rights of all Mexicans are adequately
protected.[56]

*Chapter 11*

# IN CHIAPAS,
# UNFINISHED BUSINESS

〚IIᔑᒻᓚ卪II〛〚IIᔑᒻᓚ卪II〛〚IIᔑᒻᓚ卪II〛

NEARLY TWO YEARS have passed since the Zapatistas opened a new chapter in the history of Mexico by turning the spotlight on the long invisible indigenous people of Chiapas. During all this time, Samuel Ruiz has occupied center stage not only nationally but internationally, acquiring in the process multitudes of friends and not a few additional enemies. He neglected no opportunity, at home in Chiapas, on the Mexican national scene, and internationally, to repeat a very clear message. The issues raised by the Zapatistas cannot be solved militarily. Their demands are just and urgent. The solution must be political, and it can be reached only by dialogue and discussion that will allow the growth of a national public opinion supportive of the radical social changes the situation demands.

Serious political discussion was hardly possible during the run-up to the presidential and gubernatorial elections in August 1994. Nobody on the government side was willing, or in a position, to make realistic responses to the demands of the Zapatistas. And apparently some of the Zapatista leaders hoped that the PRI would be swept from power at the elections, opening up vast new possibilities. At the time of the first National Democratic Convention just weeks before the elections, for example, Subcomandante Marcos seemed to be confident that the civil society, whose commands he promised he would henceforth obey, would topple the PRI government. This, of course, did not happen.

Perhaps the outcome would have been different if Marcos had thrown his support to Cuautémoc Cárdenas and his Revolutionary Democratic Party (PRD), which was what many had expected. But for reasons never fully explained, he chose not to do so, and the PRI was returned to power for another six years. Although the many poll watchers reported voting irregularities, the consensus both national and international was that the PRI was indeed the winner at the national level, thanks to its massive political machine.

In several states, however, including Chiapas, evidence of fraud was so strong as to raise serious questions regarding the legitimacy of the state and local officials who were declared elected. The Zapatistas immediately announced that they would not respect the official calculations that made the PRI candidate, Eduardo Robledo Rincón, the new governor of Chiapas. They warned that there would be war, not only in Chiapas but in all Mexico, if he attempted to take office in December. Many thousands of protesters held meetings, blocked roads, and occupied government and municipal offices.

The PRD, the party of Cuautémoc Cárdenas, also joined in, and their protests were coordinated with those of indigenous and campesino groups involved in land disputes. On the same day in December 1994 as the officially designated new governor of Chiapas, Eduardo Robledo, was inaugurated, PRD supporters installed their candidate, Amado Avendaño, as Governor in Rebellion. Avendaño, a lawyer and publisher of a newspaper in San Cristóbal, had been seriously injured when a truck swerved in front of his automobile during the election campaign, in what was widely believed to be an assassination attempt. Since his inauguration, Avendaño supervises a parallel state executive body in San Cristóbal, issuing instructions that he lacks the power to execute. The federal and state governments have so far not interfered.

The elections, in addition, failed to resolve internal problems of the PRI, whose control of government as a party was weakened during the previous six years. Part of the Salinas strategy designed to prepare Mexico for acceptance as a "modern state," on a par with the United States and Canada, involved the inclusion in the top-level decision-making processes of two additional actors: big business and the Catholic Church. The resulting conflict within the church has already been noted. What has now emerged is a deep division within the PRI between the modernizers and their big-business allies who support the Salinas strategy, and the so-called hardliners who would reinstate the absolute monopoly of power enjoyed by the PRI since 1929.

Evidence of the depth of this division came to light with the assassination, a month after the 1994 elections, of José Francisco Ruiz Massieu, whom President Salinas had named general secretary of the PRI just four months earlier. A former governor of Guerrero state, the slain man was the brother of the already mentioned assistant attorney general, Mario Ruiz Massieu, and he was connected by marriage to the president. Testimony of a key suspect in the killing indicated that it had been motivated by political rivalry and resistance to PRI reform. The investigation also brought to light links, stretching back through at least two Mexican administrations, between the Cali (Colombia) drug cartel, a Mexican drug cartel, and government officials.

Claiming to be unhappy with what he described as foot dragging in the investigation of his brother's assassination, Mario resigned both from his position as assistant attorney general and from the government party, the PRI. He subsequently (December 1994) received death threats for continuing independently to search for his brother's killers. A special prosecutor then named to pursue the case caused a major shock in late February 1995 when he arrested Raúl Salinas de Gortari, brother of the former president. Raúl, he said, had ordered the assassination and paid for it. The actual killer he identified as Manuel Muñoz Rocha, a PRI congressman who is a fugitive from justice.

Coming on top of the assassinations of Cardinal Posadas Ocampo (1993) and the PRI presidential candidate Luis Donaldo Colosio (1994), both also believed to be drug-related, the Ruiz Massieu killing raised questions as to the governability of the country. People even spoke openly of the "Colombianization" of Mexico.

♣

A series of provocative actions by the army and other government representatives on the edge of the Zapatista enclave further heightened tension in the weeks following the elections. Low-flying planes buzzed villages under Zapatista control. The military containment ring was strengthened, and army units repeatedly made incursions into Zapatista territory. Ejections of squatters, who had repossessed land from which politically powerful individuals had driven them, increased, as did the torturing and jailing of indigenous leaders and activists.

In this context, a second meeting of the National Democratic Convention (CND) was announced, to open in San Cristóbal in early October. It was preceded in Chiapas by a wide range of non-violent actions organized by the State Council of Campesino and Indigenous Organizations (CEOIC) and similar groups. Private lands were occupied by campesinos. Municipal buildings were seized. Prisoners went on a hunger strike. Marches and meetings were held to protest the election results and to urge the government to implement land reform and other social changes.

Although much smaller than the first CND meeting and given far less media coverage, the second gathering brought together more than a thousand representatives from all parts of Mexico. They listened in somber silence to an EZLN communiqué: "To respond to provocations, to avoid being an accomplice in the deception carried on by the government of Salinas de Cortari, not to endorse the culture of political crime that characterizes this government, and to reaffirm the commitment to the fight against fraud and imposition, the

Zapatista National Liberation Army has decided to break off the dialogue with the supreme government."

Subcomandante Marcos later clarified the communiqué, which had sounded like a declaration of war. "We didn't break off the dialogue to reignite hostilities," he told the press, "but to signal that the dialogue had bogged down. We have insisted that we are for a political and peaceful solution, but the government has chosen to favor oppression for the benefit of the powerful rather than dialogue for the benefit of the have-nots." But, he added, we are ready if the government renews the war. "Zapatista troops have finished mining all land approaches to rebel territory, and anti-aircraft units have been deployed."

Don Samuel as peace mediator was naturally disturbed by these threatening developments. He quickly made it clear, nevertheless, that he was not giving up. Let us begin over again, he said. His expanded initiative proposed a civil peace commission with ten members, new dialogues between the government and the Zapatistas, and a new government in Chiapas.

Almost simultaneously, the government's peace commissioner, Jorge Medrazo Cuéllar, whom Marcos had a short time before been criticizing for lack of effectiveness, sent a proposal to the rebels calling for a new peace commission composed both of individuals sympathetic to the Zapatistas and of members of the government's human rights commission.

All of this parleying took place against a background of mounting indigenous frustration. Thousands of angry small farmers blocked highways and occupied public buildings. They protested lack of drinking water and roads. They complained of government corruption and of the imprisonment of activists. A climate of fear in the communities close to the conflict zone produced a steady flow of refugees to the municipalities of Las Margaritas and Comitán. On October 12, fifteen thousand indigenous commemorated "the 502nd Year of Resistance" with a march through the streets of San Cristóbal. Many of them had walked from their villages for two days to participate.

Don Samuel lost no opportunity to warn the nation of the level of frustration in Chiapas and the danger of new explosions of violence. "The war in Chiapas can break out again in any place and at any time," he told the press in November. "The people see no signs of a possible solution to their problems." The danger, he insisted, is no longer just that some incident might renew fighting between the EZLN and the army. "Now the problem is everywhere."[57] He made an even more pointed criticism of the government in his sermon at a Mass for peace in San Cristóbal in December. There is a refusal, he said, "to recognize the indigenous as the emerging subjects of their own destiny." In that sermon he also said that the situation is grave "because we have today in Chiapas two states, two governments, and two armies. This is the beginning of civil war."

A week before Christmas came yet another dramatic gesture on behalf of peace. In a letter to the diocese dated December 19, Don Samuel noted a series of extremely unsettling events: municipalities that have declared themselves territory in rebellion, municipal offices occupied without bloodshed, land invasions and roadblocks in many parts of the state, the appearance in public of armed people whose statements, flags, and symbols identify them as belonging to the EZLN. "Reading these events in the light of the simplest analysis, given the explosive situation in the state and the preparations for war that can be observed, forces us to recognize that this region and the whole country are sliding down a slope leading to irreversible war and violence."[58]

Because of this situation, continued the bishop, "I have decided to have recourse to the power of penance and prayer, starting today a fast of a permanent kind in the cathedral of the diocese of San Cristóbal de Las Casas, the cathedral of peace. I invite my brother bishops, their dioceses, and all believers to join in this penitential action, asking God to move all the actors involved in the conflict to seek paths of understanding that will lead to agreement on a well-based cease-fire."

Large numbers of people in many parts of Mexico joined in the Fast for Peace that started four days before Christmas. They included retired archbishop of Oaxaca Bartolomé Carrasco Briseño and bishop of Tehuantepec Arturo Lona Reyes, as well as several public figures. Large numbers of supporters, many of them indigenous, joined Don Samuel in the cathedral in San Cristóbal, praying with him during the day and sleeping with him on the floor at night. Not all bishops approved, however, the division within the church being made public by Cardinal Adolfo Suárez Rivera of Monterrey. "The evangelical fast," he said, "should not be used as a political statement."

Without taking sides on this issue, the Mexican Bishops' Committee urged Ruiz to end his fast "in order to conserve the fullness of his faculties for the exercise of his role as mediator in the conflict in Chiapas." Others who knew that the bishop has diabetes, which could be dangerously affected by fasting, made a similar appeal. Just before the New Year, he announced that he might end his fast in a day or two, because of indications that a new and lasting truce was imminent.

A quick response to the ending of the fast was the government's recognition of the National Mediating Committee (CONAI), a group of citizens headed by Don Samuel as the impartial mediator in the conflict with the Zapatistas. For several months the government had been trying to get rid of Don Samuel as mediator, or at least to reduce his role. Jorge Madrazo had made several unsuccessful attempts to engage in direct negotiations with the Zapatistas. He had also promoted the creation of a new negotiating commission, with half of its members named by the government.

The prospects for peace thus seemed to improve significantly during the first half of January 1995, especially when Don Samuel met with Subcomandante Marcos and government representative Esteban Moctezuma Barrigán in the Lacandon jungle. Simultaneously, however, the disastrous collapse of the Mexican peso continued, forcing the government to concentrate its attention on the short-term economic situation. To complicate matters further for the government, leading bishops gave public expression to surprisingly strong criticisms of its actions and failures. And Cardinal Sandoval, as already noted, turned up new evidence in the still unsolved assassination of his predecessor, Cardinal Posadas.

Also in mid-January, the Permanent Commission of the Bishops Conference published a very negative assessment of the consequences of the economic model that had been imposed on Mexico during the Salinas presidency. It urged that those who had been illegally enriched should return the stolen goods to the state. The commission's stand was reaffirmed by Cardinal Corripio before a gathering of ten thousand people in the Basilica of Our Lady of Guadalupe. It was a striking vindication of the position Don Samuel had taken in his August 1993 letter to Pope John Paul. But it added to the general anxiety and uncertainty about the country's direction.

Involved as he was in the peace negotiations, the bishop was not forgetting his diocese. In January, in the presence of Cardinal Suárez Rivera and fifteen bishops, many of them from other countries of Latin America, he inaugurated a diocesan synod. The stated purposes of this extraordinary diocesan assembly were "to develop laws and guidelines that will establish the direction of the pastoral work of the diocese during the coming years and also to seek reconciliation among the faithful."

❖

Another event of January 1995, the collapse of the Mexican peso, had a direct negative impact on the peace process. A statement by a spokesperson for a major U.S. bank published in the *Wall Street Journal* is believed to have triggered this side effect. Mexico, he said, will have to deal with the Zapatistas before it can hope to restore confidence in the peso and obtain the international loans it needs to avoid bankruptcy. In an apparent response, President Zedillo announced in early February that the attorney general had uncovered EZLN arsenals in Mexico City and in Veracruz. In fulfillment of his constitutional duty, the president added, "in order to ensure the safety of all Mexicans and preserve social peace," he had ordered the arrest of presumed members of the EZLN. Major contingents of the armed forces were immediately moved closer to the Lacandon jungle, occupying Larraínzar, Simojovel, Ocosingo, Las Margaritas, Bochil, and other towns. Almost simultaneously, a document prepared by the intelligence section of the armed forces was released. It listed 2,275 individuals as involved with the EZLN. They included 134 members of religious orders (some Mexican and others foreigners), as well as three bishops, Samuel Ruiz, Arturo Loma Reyes (Tehuantepec), and José Luis Dibildox Martínez (Tarahumara). Houses of the Jesuits and Dominicans and of other religious orders were searched from top to bottom, as were the San Cristóbal offices of CONPAZ, the coalition of Mexican non-governmental organizations (NGOs) committed to the defense of human rights. It looked for some days as if the Mexican government was going to deal with the church in Chiapas as the Guatemalan government had dealt with the church just across the border in the early 1980s. Rumors of plans for joint operations by the Mexican and Guatemalan armies were rife.

The Zapatistas made no attempt to engage the army militarily, simply withdrawing deeper into the tropical forest as the army advanced. Dozens of suspected supporters were arrested, but they did not include any of the top leaders of the EZLN.

The government offensive provoked widespread national and international criticisms especially when it was reported that Zedillo's decision to use force had been ordered by U.S. financial interests. Protest letters published in *La Jornada,* one of the few Mexico City newspapers not controlled by the PRI, came from Nobel laureates, U.S. film makers, Italian artists, and members of Australia's parliament.

In yet another show of weakness and apparent internal dissension, the government backed off within a matter of days. Congress, on March 13, approved and the president signed the Law for Dialogue, Reconciliation, and a Dignified Peace. It formally suspended the arrest warrants against the Zapatistas and called for a new round of talks within thirty days. The government further promised that it would withdraw the soldiers from villages they had occupied in the territory that had previously been controlled by the Zapatistas.

The army offensive had caused significant hurt to the Zapatistas. It not only forced them deeper into the jungle but cut off an important part of the civilian infrastructure that provides food and logistical support for them. Nevertheless, it is generally judged that the government had been hurt more than they had by the brief attempt to find a military solution to the impasse. They had clearly not been defeated militarily, and their standing in public opinion rose significantly. An opinion poll taken in Mexico City in April showed that 75 percent of the inhabitants of the capital sympathized with them.

The army had for several days kept human rights advocates, health workers, international observers, and the media out of the territory it had occupied. That they had reasons other than military for this action soon became clear. No sooner had human rights organizations been allowed into the occupied zones than several of them began to report an upsurge of violations, including instances of torture. According to the Human Rights Center of the diocese of San Cristóbal, "Between February 10 and March 10, we documented seven cases of torture; that does not mean that this is the absolute figure, simply that it is the part we have been able to verify."[59] CONPAZ, the coalition of human rights NGOs, confirmed widespread torture, rape, arbitrary detentions, and extra-judicial killings in the twenty villages occupied by the army. Greenpeace charged that the human rights violations resulted from the application by the Mexican army of the same strategy of low intensity warfare as had been used by the Guatemalan army in its counter-insurgency campaigns, namely, a program of terrorization of the civilian population that constituted the logistical support base for the Zapatistas. Torture has long been a problem in Mexico. An Amnesty International report has called it "an endemic evil" of the Mexican system. According to the Human Rights Center of the diocese of San Cristóbal, there are several reasons for this state of affairs. Confessions extracted under torture, are — in violation of domestic law and international accords — routinely accepted by judges as evidence against the accused. Those who engage in torture are almost never punished. Torture is conducted in secret, and sophisticated techniques leave little physical evidence. According to the center, torture has usually two objectives, to extract information and to force the suspect to admit guilt and implicate others. Those tortured during the February military offensive were — according to the center's investigations — in most cases denounced to the military by the big landowners as Zapatista sympathizers. The landowners were taking advantage of the military action to harass campesinos active in the struggle to recover land that had been unjustly seized from them.

At the end of May, while discussions continued for a further round of talks, heavy troop concentrations remained in the areas from which the government had undertaken to remove them. Several times during May the Human Rights Commission of CONPAZ publicly protested the harassment by armed soldiers of villages in the municipality of Ocosingo.

❖

In the highlands of Chiapas, meanwhile, life still went on. On the valley floors and clinging precariously to the mountain slopes, a patchwork of green fields, mostly of corn, surrounded thatched-roofed farming villages. Young children played in the mud, thankful for an infrequent shower. Women in bright costumes, bent double under bundles of firewood, were photographed by tourists leaning out of the windows of their fleeting buses. The heavily armed soldiers, reminders of the unfinished business, waved the tourists past but checked other vehicles, searched young men for arms, asked people where they were going and why, and detained anyone whose papers were not in order.

The soldiers patrolled day and night. In the absence of official figures, the army was believed to have considerably upward of fifteen thousand troops in Chiapas. Subcomandante Marcos said that some fifty thousand soldiers were poised to attack. Pablo Romo, director of the Fray Bartolomé de Las Casas Human Rights Center in San Cristóbal, said he believed the number to be around twenty thousand. Reports of attacks on civilians by the army were frequent all through 1994. In late June the diocesan Human Rights Commission charged that fifty soldiers searched homes in the village of Chalam del Carmen in Ocosingo, stealing food and so terrifying the people that many of them fled to the mountains.

The crisis of the Mexican regime was highlighted when the official May Day parade in honor of the Mexican Worker was canceled in 1995. This had never happened since Mexico inaugurated the observance seventy-four years earlier. An opposition demonstration in Mexico City put an estimated eight hundred thousand workers on the streets.

Yet another shock was caused to the regime about the same time. In a bizarre twist in the investigation of the assassination of José Francisco Ruiz Massieu, his brother Mario (who earlier, as assistant attorney general, had been investigating the crime) was arrested at Newark Airport by U.S. federal authorities and charged with attempting to leave the country carrying a large quantity of dollars he had not declared. The Mexican government immediately asked for his extradition, asserting that he had accepted millions of dollars in bribes from his brother's killers, in return for which he had distorted evidence in his possession that identified Raúl Salinas de Gortari, elder brother of Carlos Salinas who was then president of Mexico, as having ordered the killing of José Francisco Ruiz Massieu.

A Federal District Court in Newark, in June 1995, denied the extradition request, the judge ruling that the Mexican government had presented evidence tainted by torture and lies. The testimony, Judge Ronald J. Hedges suggested, pointed to "political rot" within both the Mexican government and the PRI. Stories of conspiracies, violence, and shady dealings by high officials left the impression, he said, that corruption infected almost every level of government in Mexico, from the local police to Congress.

New revelations regarding the extent of corruption in the Mexican government and in the PRI are expected as additional charges against Mario Ruiz Massieu are explored. He faces a civil suit in Houston, Texas, where U.S. prosecutors seek forfeiture of more than $9 million, which they say represents bribes from drug traffickers. Further charges have also been filed against him in Mexico. He has been named along with thirteen others as having tortured suspects in the investigation, in the fall of 1994, into the assassination of his brother. And, in a separate suit, he is accused of having embezzled $750,000. Meanwhile, he is being held without bail in New Jersey.

Yet another indication of the weakened condition of the Mexican government was the unusually harsh criticism expressed by the Mexican Bishops Conference at its annual meeting in late April 1995 at the National Shrine of Our Lady of Guadalupe. At its opening session, it decided to put its prepared agenda aside and focus exclusively on the "crisis." In a statement of unparalleled strength, the bishops denounced NAFTA's free-market system as "unworkable." The "catastrophic result" of a long chain of injustices, of an economic model that is unworkable, of unemployment, of low salaries, of corruption and impunity, they said, is that forty million Mexicans are in poverty and the nation's wealth is concentrated in the hands of a privileged few. The five-day meeting denounced electoral fraud and the manipulation of information by the government through its control of radio and television and much of the press. The result, it said, is a culture characterized by a serious lack of truth, justice, and solidarity; major changes are needed in order to end corruption and to ensure respect for election results.

In addition to distancing themselves from the government, the bishops expressed stronger support of Samuel Ruiz than at any previous time in recent years. Cardinal Adolfo Suárez Rivera (Monterrey) said the government was right in calling on the Zapatistas to disarm, but it has to recognize that first of all the legitimate demands of the indigenous must be met. Attacks on Bishop Samuel Ruiz and on his role as mediator, he added, only slow down the process of building peace. According to Bishops Conference President Sergio Obeso Rivera, the fact that some indigenous took up arms has brought to light a condition of misery that is not new but rather centuries old. And the president of the conference's Commission for Social Communications insisted that the bishop of San Cristóbal has "the total support" of Mexico's bishops in his search for peace. It is clear from these developments that more and more of his fellow bishops are coming to accept Don Samuel's judgment that Mexico must do justice to its indigenous peoples, and that this cannot be done without radical changes in its political structures.

The strength of Don Samuel's position lies in the total consistency of his stand and his ability to articulate it in each changing circumstance. He gave a remarkable summing up in his Lenten pastoral letter in 1995, just as the government had decided that its brief attempt at imposing a military solution was fruitless. Our national community, he said, "is battered and broken by a war of brothers. This path of death was the result of our own wrongful behavior, in which the sin of a structurally unjust society that puts profit before human dignity is joined to egoism, social discrimination, and the drive to dominate.

"The violation of God's plan, which is a plan of life and of life in abundance, has brought on us individual and community suffering. Many communities have been displaced or evacuated, including their most unprotected members, old people, women, children. They live in acute hunger and suffer from endemic diseases. Community ties are broken. They live in fear of violence. They experience a suffering that can lead to the worst evil of all: the loss of hope and of the saving meaning of history.

"To sacrifice thousands of our brothers and sisters is judged a lesser loss than to pay the price of the substantive changes needed for the reconciliation and justice that would establish true peace.

"The voice of countless persons demands peace, but the word does not have the same meaning for everyone. While some long for peace full of changes and of hopes for their own lives and the lives of others, what some want is to return to times that are gone for ever....

"We are called today to be a space of fraternal reconciliation and pardon: a reconciliation that results from dialogue among those who recognize each other as persons with equal dignity and with the same rights, and who in consequence are ready to join together in search of the common good, rising above individual interests. This pardon must include rejection of solutions imposed by force, because we believe more in the force of truth and love that makes us accept the other as a person. It is not a passive pardon but an active one, opening roads and seeking alternative solutions when there do not seem to be any, accepting plurality of religious, cultural, and political positions, building bridges of understanding and respect to achieve unity that leads to lasting peace, laying the bases for dialogue so that together we can seek solutions that will bring us to an equitable and just order."

The issues are defined beyond any doubt. That is why Don Samuel is loved. That is why he is hated.

*Chapter 12*

# CHURCH OF THE FUTURE

||᠊ᢓᡄ᠊ᢐ|| ||᠊ᢓᡄ᠊ᢐ|| ||᠊ᢓᡄ᠊ᢐ||

T HAT DON SAMUEL has long been a threat both to powerful people in the Vatican and to the Mexican government is clear from what has already been told. Interviews and discussions with people close to him from the beginning of his work as bishop have made it possible to piece together the actions and projects that created and maintain that threat.

The Vatican's concern is twofold, theological or ecclesiological, and political. At the theological level, it questions the type of church that is being brought into existence in San Cristóbal. At the political level, it sees Don Samuel's criticism of the Mexican government's policies as hurting its strategy of creating closer ties with that government.

Enrique Dussel, the leading historian of the church in Latin America, has formulated the theological conflict in terms that help to explain where Don Samuel stands. Two models of church, Dussel says, are fighting for the soul of Latin America. One is the church of Christendom that has held sway in most of Latin America since the sixteenth century. It looks to the state to provide facilities for religious education, to pay military chaplains, to subsidize church buildings and church activities. It is a model that many bishops in Latin America still hanker after, as do many in positions of authority at the Vatican.

Challenging it is the servant church, as envisaged and promoted by Pope John XXIII. It was given its specific Latin

144

American form by liberation theology, the origin of which — Dussel insists — should not be attributed to individuals because it constitutes the reflection of a whole generation of Latin American theologians. This theology formulated the historical option for the poor, transforming the church into the church of the poor, and handing over to the people — as the main agents of history — the responsibility for their own evangelization. Bishop Ruiz stands clearly with this model of church. His entire pastorate has been dedicated to incarnating it in San Cristóbal.

The Mexican government's quarrel with the bishop arises out of his pastoral work, which has given the previously voiceless indigenous, some 80 percent of the more than one million inhabitants of the diocese, an awareness of their strength and dignity, so that they openly challenge the unjust structures of which they are the victims.

The development of the pastoral project has been gradual. Don Samuel, as we have seen, began his work as bishop within traditional concepts and formulas. He saw people who were poor, who were illiterate. He felt moved to help them. He saw himself as one who had resources he could share with them. It hardly occurred to him that they also had resources they could — and were ready to — share with him. But he was a quick learner.

Given the major problems the present papal representative, Girolamo Prigione, has created for him, it is ironic that an earlier apostolic delegate to Mexico, Archbishop Luigi Raimondi, made the suggestion that started Ruiz on the course he still follows. Raimondi urged the bishop to open schools in which to train catechists. That was in 1962.

The Marist Brothers of the Guadalupe Mission and the Sisters of the Divine Pastor were placed in charge of two schools, one for men, the other for women. The Jesuits and other religious orders also trained some catechists, but the main catechetical movement was centered for the first eight or ten years in these two schools.

The students, chosen by their own communities, came

from the mountains and the forests for courses of three or four months. The regime was like that of a seminary; the approach, the one that had been established for hundreds of years. The pupils were taught the catechism by rote, in Spanish. They learned the symbols of the liturgy and of paraliturgical devotions that were the characteristic expressions of the Catholic Church as it had evolved in Europe over more than a thousand years. The objective of the program was to transfer this "saving" knowledge through the catechists to people who were thought of as believers but living on the margin of the institutional church.

From the beginning, nevertheless, the pastoral teams charged with the running of the catechetical schools were encouraged by Don Samuel to experiment. They soon decided that it would be appropriate to present the catechism, not only in Spanish but in the indigenous languages the students spoke. The teachers went to live in the communities and began to learn the major languages. Don Samuel not only approved but set out himself to learn these languages.

What they were doing was a radical departure from centuries of missionary practice. Many thought it was a dangerous turning away from tradition. But at the Vatican Council, Don Samuel found other bishops who were questioning the traditional approach to evangelization and who insisted on the need for daring experimentation. He was strengthened to continue on the road he had chosen. Over the years he maintained and expanded the contacts he made in Rome with bishops from Latin America, Africa, and Asia in whose dioceses were large numbers of people belonging to non-European cultures. The result was a progressive development of new missionary approaches based on a scientific understanding of communication processes.

As the pastoral teams learned the indigenous languages, they became aware of the overtones carried by the words they were using, words that they had assumed had the same meaning for their pupils as they had for themselves. Gradually they came to see that there lay before them the huge task of restating in the indigenous languages the Christian message that had been entrusted to them in Spanish. So they began to have the catechists translate into their languages hymns that they had traditionally been taught in Spanish. Then, bit by bit, came translations of the Scriptures. Full integration into the Christian community no longer required knowledge of a foreign language.

Xochitl Leyva Solano, a social scientist who has made an extensive study of the political, social, and religious awakening of the indigenous of Chiapas, stresses the importance of the translation of the Bible into their languages.[60] As the Book of Exodus was being translated into Tzeltal between 1972 and 1974, it provoked discussions in the communities about freedom, faith, hope, and love. At first, the missionaries summed up the reflections, but gradually the catechists took on this function. The result was a catechism written in Tzeltal, *We Are Seeking Freedom*.

This book is more an analysis, in the light of faith, of the social situation of the people who wrote it than a catechism in the conventional sense. "It is God's will that we get rid of everything that oppresses us. The Word of God tells us that as a community we should set out in search of liberty. If we seek improvement and liberty, God will accompany us. When the Israelites lived as slaves, they had to go out and fight to win their liberty. When our forefathers lived as day laborers, they had to fight together to obtain their land. They were people of great faith. True liberty has not yet come. We have to build up strength in our hearts and fight and suffer for a long time still. We have to fight against poverty, hunger, and injustice."

The Tzeltal catechism also reflects on "the new man" as envisaged by St. Paul. "The new man is not a man alone but a man in community, united with all his friends by the Spirit. All together, we constitute a single thought, a single work, a single heart with the same hope."

All this input from the people was helping the members of the diocesan pastoral teams to become aware of the vast body of knowledge stored in the collective memory of the Mayan people. One of the first things they noticed was their prodigious memory. "We were amazed," one commented, "when we found they could repeat word for word a homily that Don Samuel had preached." Many could recite long passages of the Popol Vuh, the centuries-old beliefs that constituted the core of the self-understanding of the Mayan people, their creation myth, their sacred doctrines, their prophetic visions. All of this was not retained by mechanical memory, but internalized and reformulated in terms calculated to make it meaningful to each generation, as happens with the myths of all oral cultures. As the pastoral teams came to an awareness and appreciation of the vast intellectual and emotional resources stored behind what were once for them blank faces, they gradually developed a better understanding of their own role in the process of evangelization.

❖

In this process, it early became clear that the community had to play a vital part. All life, religious, social, economic, and political, was communitarian, and communities were of many kinds. A farming community might consist of as few as a dozen families, and it might count two hundred or more. The older communities tended to be stable social units, speaking one language, wearing the same clothing, identified with the land on which they lived. When the population pressure in the highlands forced many in the 1970s to move into the Lacandon jungle, this changed. Usually a homogeneous group would set out from a given community, but in the jungle they would find themselves working with people of different languages and customs, so that life there has become more diversified within a generic homogeneity. But in every situation, the socialization was such that all important decisions were made by the community, and the decision-making processes were determined by a universally shared code of conduct handed down from each generation to the next.

As the pastoral teams came to realize that they were touching a world whose ways of thinking and deciding were radically different from their own, the need for highly skilled interpreters of this reality became obvious. Don Samuel responded by having members of these teams take courses in anthropology, communications, and other appropriate sciences at the Universidad Iberoamericana, the Jesuit university in Mexico City.

One of the things these experts discovered had very important consequences. Following their own assumptions as to what was appropriate, the pastoral teams selected the candidates, designated the newly trained catechists as the official representatives of the diocese in their communities, and paid them a salary. To their amazement, they discovered that this severely limited the influence of the catechists. It converted them into employees of an outside institution, with the result that they achieved no status within the community. They were outsiders.

The social structure of the indigenous community is determined by *cargos*. A *cargo* is a commitment to perform a service to the community as a member of a traditional religious association or confraternity. There is a hierarchy of *cargos*, starting with the *mayordomo* or *martoma* and moving up through flag carriers, *alguaciles* ("sheriffs"), and other duties, to presiders. The entire process exists to ensure proper celebration of each community's religious festivals, festivals around which the social life of the community revolves. Each community will have several major festivals, celebrating the particular saint with whom it identifies and to whom it looks for protection, as well as Holy Week, All Saints, Corpus Christi, and one or two feasts of the Virgin Mary.

For each of these festivals, there exists a kind of confraternity that is responsible for the proper preparations, including the provision of generous supplies of food and drink. The key concept is that of community service. By service, one wins respect and authority. Those who take their commitment seriously move upward through the hierarchy of service to become finally the *Tatic*, the honorary father of the entire community. The men who reach that summit of honor are called *Tatiletic;* the women, *Mailetic.* And if one dies while performing this highest level of service, one becomes semi-divinized as *Maitateletic* or *Tatilmailetic* ("mother/father; father/mother"), that is to say, one transcends gender.

As the pastoral teams began more and more to understand and appreciate the value of these community structures and beliefs, they came to recognize that the catechists could perform their function more fully and achieve the social rewards of their service by becoming more closely identified with the traditional forms of service. This meant, among other things, that they were no longer paid for their services.

Far from slowing down the rush of volunteers, this change increased it dramatically. The number of catechists had already grown in less than a decade from the original handful to some six hundred. Now they started to increase exponentially, so that by the mid-1990s they numbered at least eight thousand, a presence of official church workers unparalleled in any diocese in the Catholic world.

❖

A major advance took place in 1968. In consultation with his staff, Don Samuel decided to ask a cross-section of community leaders to perform an evaluation of the work of the diocese among the indigenous. A committee of thirty was formed. They did not read or write, nor did they speak Spanish, but all were known and respected for their services to their communities and for their wisdom. After three months of discussions both in San Cristóbal and in the communities, they offered their opinions in the form of questions.

"The God you proclaim to us," they said, "is a God that appeals to us because he exhibits two qualities: he is a God who liberates and a God who loves. But there is one issue we want clarified. Does this God of yours know how to save bodies, or is he concerned only with saving souls?"

Second question. "You tell us that, according to the Bible, the Word of God is like a seed that is to be found everywhere, and that it is already a seed of salvation. If that is so, can we not assume that these seeds are also to be found where we live in the mountains and the forests? In that case, why should we have to come to your centers, to your schools, to seek those seeds and to harvest them? Why cannot we do it in our own communities?"

A final question. "You have lived among us and shared our lives. We regard you as our brothers and sisters. Is it your desire to be our brothers and sisters for all time?"

As the diocesan pastoral teams analyzed these three questions and reflected on them, they saw entirely new perspectives open before them. They came to understand what the Vatican Council meant when it said the seeds of the Word were already present in every culture. The first task of the evangelizer was to look for those seeds already present in the cultures and in the history of each people. The next step was to incorporate the Christian message into the saving truth that was already part of the lives of the indigenous.

One immediate result was to replace the catechetical centers in San Cristóbal with centers in each of the language regions. This change played a big part in the already mentioned increase in the number of catechists. It occurred at the same time as the exodus of people from the highlands of Chiapas to settle in the Lacandon jungle. The diocesan priests, sisters, and lay workers went with them, sharing the hardships of the pioneers and forging ever stronger bonds of identification. Many of them remember that experience as their moment of conversion, their awakening to a new understanding of their vocation.

The reminder that Christianity was not a disincarnate religion, that it should be concerned with bodies as well as souls, also brought concrete results. Multipurpose teams were formed to develop projects of many kinds in the villages: cooperatives, agricultural education, literacy programs, health care. The communities were encouraged to take initiatives, and they became conscious of their own potential to change their lives.

The logic of all these developments led to the exploration of further ways of liturgical presence in the many remote communities that were visited only infrequently by a priest. It was decided to authorize the *tuhuneletic* to perform the functions that in the Latin rite normally belong to the deacon. *Tuhunel* in Tzeltal, Tzotzil, and Tojolabal means "servant." One of the services now carried out by the *tuhuneletic* is to take hosts consecrated by a priest to the villages for a service of the Word that includes distribution of the consecrated hosts to the people.

All this empowerment of the indigenous of the diocese has understandably upset the Europeanized, Spanish-speaking people, the *criollos* and *ladinos* who had long enjoyed the primary attention of the church and who had been accustomed to using the clergy as legitimators of the privileges they enjoyed. Many of them resist the idea of a preferential option by the church for the poor, notwithstanding the fact that this was formally proclaimed by the bishops of Latin America at their meeting in Puebla in 1979 and reaffirmed at the more recent meeting in Santo Domingo in 1992. Even harder for them to accept is Don Samuel's insistence that the highest preference must go to the indigenous because they are the poorest of the poor.

In addition to such self-interested people, there are some within the clerical ranks who are disturbed by the radical reshaping of church structures, the radical realignment of lines of power, the radical democratization of a church that for more than a thousand years has worn the dress of absolute monarchy. They have included some, albeit surprisingly few, of the pastoral workers of the diocese of San Cristóbal. Don Samuel has had the skills and the leadership qualities to carry with him on his revolutionary road the overwhelming majority of his co-workers. It is impossible to spend any length of time in the diocese without becoming aware of the extraordinary *esprit de corps* of the large family of professional diocesan workers, lay and clerical. They are a diverse group of people, including volunteers from many parts of the world drawn to San Cristóbal by the enthusiastic reports of meaningful apostolic work from others who have preceded them. They work happily, often with little material comfort, not seldom with threats to their well-being and their lives. All that is a testimony that cannot be ignored.

❖

A few malcontents, nevertheless, can create a lot of problems. The Roman curia never accepted the program of reform mandated by the Vatican Council. While lip service must be given to renewal, the efforts to return to the church of Pius XII, or even to that of Pius IX have intensified during the present pontificate. The Congregation for the Doctrine of the Faith under the leadership of Cardinal Joseph Ratzinger hunts for heretics with the same enthusiasm that once marked the Inquisition. This atmosphere of suspicion in Rome regarding all innovations ensures that the complaints of malcontents are given a sympathetic hearing, especially if these malcontents are persons with money and power, as is true of many of Don Samuel's critics in Chiapas and elsewhere in Mexico.

According to Papal Nuncio Prigione, the charges against Don Samuel forwarded to Rome were that he was guilty of grave errors as regards Catholic doctrine, pastoral practice, and administration of the diocese. No specifics have ever been officially made public. Of the three areas identified, undoubtedly the most serious for a bishop, who is charged with teaching doctrine, is the accusation that he is guilty of doctrinal error.

Don Samuel's enemies in Mexico focus on his denunciations of the institutionalized injustice to which the indigenous are subjected. What he is really doing, they insist, is promoting the Marxist-inspired class warfare that follows logically from his commitment to the theology of liberation.

That the spirit of the theology of liberation infuses the work of the diocese of San Cristóbal is clear. The panel of indigenous leaders chosen in 1968 to evaluate the pastoral workers were quite clear about that, as demonstrated by their question whether God is concerned only with saving souls and not also with saving bodies. But it must be noted that in 1968, the theology of liberation had not yet received a name. Gustavo Gutiérrez's groundbreaking book would not appear until three years later. What we see here seems to be the parallel growth of ideas triggered by new social situations. Clearly, the indigenous of Chiapas had not drawn their inspiration from Marx. More widely, the impact of Marxist thought on the diocese of Chiapas has been neither more or less than its impact in the entire Third World. Like Pasteur, like Freud, Marx and the science of sociology of which he was a founder are part of the culture of the twentieth century. They influence the thinking of Cardinal Ratzinger, head of the Congregation for the Doctrine of the Faith, no less than the bishop of San Cristóbal. The cardinal will have difficulty in establishing that this constitutes a grave doctrinal error.

The pastoral practice and style of government of Don Samuel have, unquestionably, been extremely innovative. Decision-making has been democratized to an impressive extent. Serious efforts have been made to identify in the cultures of the Mayan peoples the "seeds of the Word" that Vatican II declared to be present in all cultures.

This approach stands in clear contrast to the entire history of evangelization in Latin America. Hernán Cortés, who in 1519 led the Spanish military operation that overthrew the Aztec empire, set out what became the generally accepted method. The first step, he said, was "the extirpation of idolatry." Most of the missionaries had a similar obsession with idolatry. They regarded all religious practices of the people they encountered as the work of the devil, and they had no hesitation in using the Spanish soldiers to destroy places of worship, objects of devotion or reverence, and even sacred books. It was only when the people and the land had been purged of all of these works of the devil, they believed, that the task of conversion to the true faith could begin.

Nobody would today attempt to justify that approach. It

is rejected not only by the consensus of the contemporary world on every person's right to free expression of religious beliefs, but more concretely by the Second Vatican Council. In its Decree on the Missionary Activity of the Church, it stated emphatically that "the seeds of the Word" are to be found in all religions. The Declaration on the Relationship of the Church to Non-Christian Religions contains an expanded version of the same concept.

"From ancient times down to the present," it reads, "there has existed among diverse peoples a certain perception of that hidden power which hovers over the course of things and over the events of human life; at times, indeed, recognition can be found of a Supreme Divinity and of a Supreme Father too. Such a perception and such a recognition instill the lives of these peoples with a profound religious sense."

A better historical comprehension of the psychologies of different cultures has also helped people like Don Samuel to understand how we should approach the evangelization of indigenous peoples. The point is well made by historian Juan Schobinger. "In general terms, pre-Columbian religious ideas and practices can be said to be closely connected to a worldview diametrically opposed to our own: intuitive, open to nature and the cosmos rather than shut up in the ego, communitarian rather than individualistic, seeing everything visible as a symbol of something greater, on which they depended. America — particularly in its high cultures — represents a notable conservation of the magical-mythical mentality that forms one of the great steps in the cultural evolution of the human race. So the collision that occurred in the sixteenth century was not just between opposing cultures, or between races, or between different historical products; it was not between 'more advanced' and 'backward' cultures, or 'civilized' people and 'barbarians.' It was, essentially, between two states of consciousness, and this is perhaps why it was so painful."[61]

❖

Another aspect of Don Samuel's pastoral practice, however, is undoubtedly looked on with suspicion by many in the Roman curia. The process of decentralization of decision-making and the upgrading of the status and expansion of the roles of the catechists and the *tuhuneletic*, what he himself has called the de-Europeanization and the declericalization of the diocese, is revolutionary. Its logical conclusion is the formation of a new rite in the church. There are, indeed, many rites in the Catholic Church, each of them of the same dignity and authority as the Latin rite. But all of them go back to early days of Christianity, and Rome has always tried and continues to try to downgrade their importance and force them to conform to its structures, practices, and controls. The idea of a new rite for the poorest of the Third World's poor is beyond the Roman imagination. Perish the thought!

Intimately related to the notion of a new rite is the issue of clerical celibacy. Don Samuel is deeply convinced that the church structures should follow the pattern of the traditional structures that undergird community life. Within this concept, the ascent to the role of religious and spiritual leader is clearly defined. He or she begins with the most modest *cargo*, that of *mayordomo*, and ascends over many years to that of presider — presider in principle not only at social ceremonies but at the Eucharist. As far back as the 1974 Indigenous Congress, one of the specific demands was for indigenous priests. Now, an important element in the traditional progress toward the role of presider is the lifestyle of the candidate. As a general rule indeed, a man must be married to be given a *cargo*, and traditionally the wife is included in the discharge of the *cargo*. The wife of the *alguacil*, for example, would be addressed as *Señora Alguacil*. This has carried over to the office of *tuhunel*. The wife is often called on to accompany her husband at official functions, sometimes also called on alone to visit and to pray with or for the sick or troubled. That the ministry is assumed by the couple, not just the man, offers an insight into the dignity and role of the woman among the indigenous of Chiapas.

Preparation for the office — the *cargo* — of ordained minister must obviously be very different in this culture from the practice of isolation in a seminary and a commitment to perpetual celibacy that is standard in the Roman rite of Catholicism. If the priesthood is something to be conferred in recognition of a life of service to the community, there is no room for celibates.

Don Samuel is fully aware of the roadblock. More than once he has indicated that he would like to ordain to the priesthood such community leaders. What stops him is his commitment to the church of which he forms a part. He has made it abundantly clear that he will not break ranks. He will obey whatever orders he receives from Rome. He has, nevertheless, made it equally clear that he wants and hopes for change. That is a very modest and humble stand. But in an atmosphere in which Rome demands an assent of the will on every position on which the pope has declared himself, is it enough?

❖

In addition to — and perhaps more important than — Don Samuel's "doctrinal, pastoral, and administrative" errors, he must confront the political maneuvers designed to have Rome remove him or at least impose restraints that will effectively neutralize him. Since these involve principally the Mexican government and the Chiapan power brokers, it is necessary to examine how the bishop has offended them.

Although the initiative for the 1974 Congress of the Indigenous came — as already described — from the governor of the state of Chiapas, the direction this assembly took was determined overwhelmingly by the catechists who participated in its preparation. Nearly the entire indigenous population of Chiapas deliberated over a year and then selected two thousand delegates — most of them catechists — to represent them in the congress.

The congress was the moment when the Mexican government realized the threat represented by the new approach to evangelization of the diocese of San Cristóbal. It revealed the existence of an organized and informed people conscious of their rights and no longer willing to accept crumbs instead of justice. The challenge was twofold. It was to the vested interests of the small elite who own most of the land and control the economy of Chiapas. The demands of the indigenous, particularly as voiced by the Zapatistas in 1994, would mean an end to privilege. But it was also a challenge to their status. Hitherto, they alone had the right to speak and to decide. They were "the people of reason." Now the less-than-human "Indians" wanted to be treated as equals. What intolerable effrontery!

The threat was not only to Chiapas. Ever since the 1974 Indigenous Conference, the federal government was aware of the new self-perception of the indigenous peoples of Chiapas. It was also aware that the new mood was contagious, that it could spread to the many other states with a substantial indigenous population, that the entire system was being challenged.

The challenge came at a bad time for the Party of the Institutionalized Revolution (PRI). In power since the late 1920s, it had long since succumbed to the corruption that inevitably follows absolute power. Election rigging, graft, bribery, human rights abuses, and drug dealing were widespread. Private armies protected the lands stolen from the indigenous and the peasants by the powerful. Frequently, the federal army joined in intimidating and terrorizing the campesinos.

In the early 1990s, as part of its strategy to win admission to the North American Free Trade Agreement (NAFTA), the government had enacted constitutional reforms. Amendments to Article 27 included, among other things, a provision that no further petitions for *ejido* land distribution would be accepted, a change that particularly affected Chiapas where the land reform demanded by the 1917 Constitution had never been implemented.

Another constitutional amendment eliminated most of the

legal restrictions that had affected the institutional Catholic Church since 1917. By this action, the government hoped to win a double award: to get the Mexican bishops to approve of NAFTA and to present to the world a modern face as a country ready to bury old quarrels.

The government project had the solid backing of the papal representative, Girolamo Prigione. An ambitious cleric, he had worked hard for years to secure both this constitutional amendment and the establishment of full diplomatic relations — with himself as nuncio — between the Holy See and the Mexican government. Mexico was for him, as for like-minded members of the Roman curia, the base from which to launch a new evangelization of Latin America. With the aid of Lumen 2000 and similar tele-evangelizing systems, they were confident they could create a neo-Christendom that would once more make Rome the center of the world.

Prigione and the PRI both saw the August 1993 visit to Mexico of Pope John Paul II as an opportunity to cement their alliance and advance their respective agendas. The program was carefully orchestrated, both to demonstrate the new happy relations of church and state and to present Mexico as having moved from the Third to the First World, an event to be solemnized within months by the inauguration of NAFTA.

Don Samuel was faced with a crisis of conscience. Thanks to his network of pastoral workers spread throughout the diocese, he knew the thinking of his people. For them, the recent constitutional amendment, which effectively put an end to the *ejido* system of landholding, meant that when NAFTA came into effect, they would be destroyed. The bishop and his associates agreed with this analysis. They had reached the conclusion that there would be no justice for the poor as long as the corrupt PRI controlled the federal government. They could no longer deal simply with the effects in their own area. They had to challenge the systemic causes.

The result was the already analyzed pastoral letter "In This

Hour of Grace," hand-delivered by the bishop to the pope when he visited Mérida, Yucatán. In addition to denouncing NAFTA, it openly charged the federal government with corruption, involvement at high levels in drug dealing, repression in the countryside and in the towns, and election rigging. It was an action that took extraordinary courage. The bishop knew that he was putting his entire career at risk. He also knew that he was exposing himself to the danger of assassination. But this was for him the moment when he had to justify his stewardship. And he knew that his pastoral workers were 100 percent with him.

The campaign to oust Don Samuel that followed was obviously orchestrated by the Mexican government and the nuncio. All indications, as 1993 approached its end, were that San Cristóbal would soon have a new bishop, or — at least — that a coadjutor bishop with final power of decision would be imposed.

The Zapatista uprising on New Year's Day 1994, as we have seen, altered the equation. The Mexican government was forced to recognize that it needed Samuel Ruiz. In consequence, as long as the stalemate would continue, the Vatican dogs had to be held in leash.

In leash, yes, but not called off. Were the Mexican government to resolve the crisis, either by negotiations or by force, there would most likely be renewed efforts to oust Don Samuel. And how long can the stalemate continue? From the outset, this has constituted an utterly anomalous situation — a sovereign government negotiating with a handful of armed rebels.

There is, nevertheless, no easy solution for the government. It has already made one attempt at a military solution. But a military solution remains unlikely. Quite apart from the negative international reaction to a probably extended military operation, the Mexican armed forces are widely believed to have neither the morale nor the training to conduct a jungle war. And a change in public opinion in the United States would seem to exclude U.S. military involvement on the scale of the support provided in the 1980s to the Nicaraguan contras and to the Salvadoran armed forces.

In addition, there is the belief of both parties to the conflict in Chiapas that time is on their side. The government does not have the resources to resolve the conflict by acceding to the Zapatista demands. That would require a social revolution at least as radical as that of the second decade of this century. Instead, it is counting on its proven approach of splitting the opposition by buying off some of the leaders. Its welfare agencies are busy in the Chiapan countryside dispensing favors to its supporters. The Zapatistas, for their part, feel confident that they can survive indefinitely in their jungle fastnesses. They hope that the already widespread support, both within Mexico and internationally, will continue to grow, as the social conditions in the country deteriorate.

In these circumstances, the impasse could continue for years. Prigione will be seventy-five in 1997, the age at which bishops submit their resignation. He will be very disappointed if he does not soon get a cardinal's hat in recognition of his diplomatic efforts in the service of the Holy See; and that would mean his departure from Mexico to take up residence in Rome. Transfer would not necessarily mean that he would no longer have a voice in determining Don Samuel's future, but it would as a minimum mean that he would have less interest in helping the Mexican government. In addition, the climate in Rome might change significantly in two or three years.

Prigione kept a low public profile all through 1995. Don Samuel, for his part, continued throughout the summer and fall his struggle to keep the faltering peace process alive, while the Mexican government tried one stratagem after another to eliminate him from the process. It proposed, for example, to substitute a new body, the Commission of Concord and Pacification (COCOPA), made up of legislators from the various political parties, for the National Mediating Committee (CONAI) that he heads. The Zapatistas insisted on dealing only with CONAI, and the impasse was finally solved by bringing both groups into the discussions. This was a partial victory for the government, enabling it to weaken Don Samuel's position by representing CONAI not as impartial but as speaking for the Zapatistas.

In spite of such ambiguities, CONAI continued to advance the peace process. Thanks to its pressures, representatives of the government and of the Zapatistas met six times at San Andrés Larraínzar between April and September 1995. The atmosphere of these talks was frequently hostile, with the Zapatista delegates protesting the continued militarization of the state of Chiapas and the harassment of the civilian population by the army. Nevertheless, agreement was finally reached on a list of issues on which substantive discussions are to be held, though without a timetable for completion of this process. Heading the list are indigenous culture and rights, democracy and justice, development and welfare, and women's rights in Chiapas. Further down on the agenda are still more contentious subjects: political and social participation of the EZLN, military detente, and class reconciliation in Chiapas.

Also during the summer of 1995, the government moved against Don Samuel on another front. Between June and September seven foreign priests working in the diocese of San Cristóbal were either expelled or denied re-entry after brief visits abroad, and two other foreign priests and three nuns were ordered to leave the country. No formal charges were brought. Permission for foreigners to enter or stay in Mexico is at the complete discretion of the federal authorities. But officials charged that the reason for the action was that these priests and sisters were engaged in politics and sympathizing with the Zapatistas.

At this point the hand of Nuncio Prigione was again seen. On August 14, Raúl Vera López, bishop of Ciudad Altamirano (Guerrero), was named coadjutor to Bishop Samuel Ruiz. The pope, according to canon law, can at his discretion appoint a coadjutor, with right of succession and the other rights and obligations "established in his letter of appointment," to any diocese.

Don Samuel and his pastoral team have put the best face on the appointment, welcoming the addition to the team and promising full cooperation. Other observers had more mixed reactions. On the positive side, Prigione's campaign to remove Don Samuel from San Cristóbal has failed. This was placed on the record on August 18 by a statement signed by Hector González Martínez, archbishop of Antequera (Oaxaca). Antequera is the ecclesiastical province to which the diocese of San Cristóbal belongs. "We are pleased," he wrote, "that after much discernment, study, and analysis of information received — and after having listened to Don Samuel and carrying out pertinent consultations — the Holy Father has decided to confirm our brother Don Samuel as diocesan bishop."

On the other hand, the extent to which he will be able to pursue his life work for the integral liberation, material and spiritual, of the indigenous of his diocese remains to be seen. The authority of the coadjutor, as set out in his letter of appointment, has not been officially disclosed, but a hint of his powers was given by Nuncio Prigione. Vera López, he said, would handle the negotiations with the government concerning the five priests and pastoral workers who have been ordered to leave, because "Samuel Ruiz is no longer responsible for the clergy in the diocese."[62]

At a press conference in which he was joined by Don Samuel, Bishop Vera López said his principal task would be "to promote unity" and to strengthen "the mystery of communion which the church should always have."[63] The cattle ranchers and other power brokers of Chiapas understandably interpreted this as a confirmation of their charges that Don Samuel was the cause of division in the San Cristóbal church. At the press conference, Vera López further revealed his concerns by condemning what he called the "Marxist element" of liberation theology.

According to the prestigious London-based *Latin Ameri-*

*can Weekly Report* (September 14, 1995), the appointment of Vera López (whom it describes as Nuncio Prigione's "hatchet man") is a pay-off by the Vatican to the Mexican government for its removal of constitutional restrictions on the church. Vera López, it says, shares little of Ruiz's outlook and many of the views of Mexico's security chiefs.

"The Vatican's intention is to begin silently and gradually to dismantle the pastoral line of the diocese, according to Enrique Dussel, a founder and longtime president of the Commission for the Study of Church History in Latin America. Secret instructions given to Bishop Vera by the Vatican Congregation for Bishops, Dussel said, include control of the diocesan seminary and the appointment and removal of priests. This means that "administratively and bureaucratically the Vatican has taken away a large part of Don Samuel's powers."[64]

The ambiguity about the coadjutor's role and intentions introduces a further element of uncertainty into the ongoing diocesan synod. A synod is a legislative assembly for a diocese. Its role is to evaluate the current state of religion and to make decisions calculated to promote good order and active evangelization. Under the current Code of Canon Law, the bishop of the diocese calls it and chooses its members. Discussion is free, but the bishop is the sole legislator. At the close, he sends the legislation enacted and any declarations to the archbishop of the province to which the diocese belongs or to the national bishops conference. The announcement at the end of 1994 of plans to hold a synod made it clear that its purpose was to formalize the restructuring that has been effected over thirty-five years in San Cristóbal. Only the future can determine whether and to what extent the appointment of a coadjutor may affect this intention.

Meanwhile, one thing is definite. The response of Don Samuel and his fellow workers to the naming of the coadjutor makes it perfectly clear that they intend, in communion with the local and universal church, to continue the project of evangelization to which they have been committed for thirty-five years, a project the entire diocese formally adopted at a general assembly a decade ago. "Our diocesan church, in union with both the Universal and Latin American Church, proclaims the life and work of Jesus in a fraternal and participatory community dedicated to and serving the people. Like Jesus, it immerses itself in the process of the liberation of the oppressed, in which they become the authors of their own history and through which we, together, build a new society that anticipates God's reign."[65]

# NOTES

1. "Declaración de la Selva Lacandona, 'Hoy decimos ¡Basta!' " *La Jornada* (Mexico City), January 2, 1994.

2. "¿Nos van a perdonar...?" *El Financiero* (Mexico City), January 21, 1994.

3. Canadian Catholic Organization for Development and Peace, press release, Montreal, January 1994; *America's Watch Report* 6, no. 3 (March 1, 1994); Amnesty International report on January 15–25, 1994, mission to Chiapas, London, 1994.

4. *Proceso* (Mexico City) 923 (July 11, 1994): 34.

5. Text of 1994 Lenten Pastoral Letter in *CENCOS* (Mexico City), March 1994.

6. "Declaración de la Selva Lacandona."

7. *Proceso* (Mexico City) 923 (July 11, 1994): 34.

8. Evon Z. Vogt, "Possible Sacred Aspects of the Chiapas Rebellion," *Cultural Survival Quarterly* (Spring 1984): 34.

9. "La Diócesis de San Cristóbal de Las Casas durante los últimos xxv años," Centro Regional de Informaciones Ecuménicas A.C. (Mexico City), Documento 28–29 (January 1984/February 1985).

10. Michael Tangeman, *Mexico at the Crossroads: Politics, the Church, and the Poor* (Maryknoll, N.Y.: Orbis Books, 1995), 9.

11. Philip J. Russell, *The Chiapas Rebellion* (Austin, Tex.: Mexico Resource Center, 1995), 7.

12. Gary H. Gossen, "Comments on the Zapatista Movement," *Cultural Survival Quarterly* (Spring 1994): 19–21.

13. *Proceso* (Mexico City) 901 (February 17, 1994): 25.

14. Russell, *The Chiapas Rebellion*, 32.

15. Ruiz letter to Pope John Paul II, August 6, 1993, in *CENCOS* (Mexico City), September 1993.

16. *Plan diocesano,* Diocese of San Cristóbal, Chiapas, 1986, 39.

17. Ibid., 5–23.

18. *La Jornada* (Mexico City), September 23, 1991.

19. *¡Gloria a Dios en los cielos y en la tierra paz a quienes ama el Señor!* San Cristóbal, December 1993.

20. *International Miami Herald,* March 13, 1994.

21. Philip J. Russell, *The Chiapas Rebellion* (Austin, Tex.: Mexico Resource Center, 1995), 11.

22. *El Financiero* (Mexico City), January 30, 1994.

23. Ibid., 9.

24. Andrés Aubry, *San Cristóbal de Las Casas: Su historia urbana, demográfica y monumental, 1528-1990* (San Cristóbal de Las Casas: INAREMAC, 1991).

25. *El Financiero* (Mexico City), International Edition, July 11-17, 1994, 3.

26. *La Jornada* (Mexico City), September 25, 1991, 17.

27. Carlos Fazio, "Wojtyla y los Indios de Chiapas," *El Financiero* (Mexico City), January 31, 1994.

28. Luisa Reyes in *La Jornada,* September 25, 1991.

29. *Proceso* (Mexico City) 900 (January 31, 1994): 24.

30. *CENCOS/Iglesias* (Mexico City), February 1992, 3.

31. Personal communication to author from JoséÁlvarez Icaza of CENCOS (Mexico City), May 29, 1995.

32. English translation in *Origins* (USCC, Washington, D.C.) 23, no. 34 (February 10, 1994).

33. Miguel Angel Granados Chapa, *El Financiero* (Mexico City), October 24, 1993.

34. *Proceso* (Mexico City) 875 (August 9, 1993): 6.

35. Ibid.

36. *Excelsior* (Mexico City), August 27, 1994.

37. *Proceso* (Mexico City) 926 (August 1, 1994): 33.

38. Ibid., 899 (January 24, 1994): 30.

39. Ibid., 926 (August 1, 1994): 33.

40. *El Financiero* (Mexico City), October 24, 1994.

41. *CENCOS/Iglesias* (Mexico City), November 1993, 13.

42. "Update from Vivian in Mexico," report dated November 7, 1993, from Sister Vivian Coulan, a pastoral worker in the diocese of San Cristóbal.

43. *Chiapas: The Rebellion of the Excluded* (Washington, D.C.: EPICA, 1994), 5.

44. Ibid., 12.

45. Philip J. Russell, *The Chiapas Rebellion* (Austin, Tex.: Mexico Resource Center, 1995), 70.

46. *Proceso* (Mexico City) 928 (August 15, 1995): 38.

47. *Envío* (Instituto Histórico Centroamericano, Managua, Nicaragua) 13, no. 155 (June 1994).

48. *Siglo XXI* (Mexico City), March 9, 1994.

49. Press Conference for group organized by CENCOS, Washington, D.C., San Cristóbal, July 24, 1994.

50. *La Jornada* (Mexico City), June 12, 1994.

51. *Dial* (Diffusion de l'Information sur l'Amérique latine, Paris), no. 1485 (April 26, 1990): 7.

52. *Plan diocesano*, San Cristóbal, 1986, 1.

53. "O surgimento do tradicionalismo na teologia latino-americana," *Revista Eclesiástica Brasileira*, March 1980.

54. *Oiga* (Lima), January 1984; *30 Giorni* (Rome), March 1984; *Neue Ordnung*, August 1984.

55. For a fuller discussion of these issues, see Gary MacEoin, *Unlikely Allies: The Christian-Socialist Convergence* (New York: Crossroad, 1990), 91.

56. *Proceso* (Mexico City) 923 (July 11, 1994): 32.

57. *La Jornada* (Mexico City), November 13, 1994.

58. *CENCOS/Iglesias* (Mexico City), December 1994, 2.

59. *Tortura: ¿Estado de Derecho?* Centro de Derechos Humanos "Fray Bartolomé de Las Casas," Chiapas, 1995. See also by same Center: *En la ausencia de justicia: Informe semestral julio a diciembre de 1993* (n.d.), and *Informe preliminar de violaciones a los derechos humanos en Chiapas del 9 de febrero al 9 de abril de 1995* (1995).

60. *Proceso* (Mexico City) 901 (February 7, 1994): 22.

61. Enrique Dussel, ed., *The Church in Latin America, 1492–1992* (Maryknoll, N.Y.: Orbis Books, 1992), 23.

62. *La Jornada* (Mexico City), October 11 and 17, 1995.

63. *CENCOS/Iglesias* (Mexico City), September 1995.

64. *Proceso* (Mexico City) 981 (August 21, 1995): 20.

65. *Plan diocesano*, Diocese of San Cristóbal, Chiapas, 1986, 39.

# INDEX

170